Paperbacks on Musicology
6

Paperbacks on Musicology
Edited by Andrew D. McCredie
In Collaboration with Richard Schaal

6

HEINRICHSHOFEN EDITION
NEW YORK

WULF KONOLD

The String Quartet

From its Beginnings to Franz Schubert

Translated by
Susan Hellauer

HEINRICHSHOFEN EDITION
NEW YORK

Sole Selling Agents:
C. F. Peters Corporation — 373 Park Avenue South, New York, N.Y. 10016

Library of Congress Cataloging in Publication Data

Konold, Wulf.
   The string quartet, from its beginnings to Franz
Schubert.

   (Paperbacks on musicology ; 6)
   Translation of: Das Streichquartett, von den
Anfängen bis Franz Schubert.
   Bibliography: p.
   Discography: p.
   Includes index.
   1. String quartet. I. Title. II. Series.
ML1160.K6513 1984   785.7'0471   84-12927
ISBN 3-7959-0345-9 (pbk.)

Sole Selling Agents:
C.F.Peters Corporation - 373 Park Avenue South, New York, N.Y.10016

Contents

Foreword

The history and esthetics of the string quartet, quite apart from its historical performance practice and appreciation, have not been presented comprehensively in the last fifty years (at least not in Germany), since Wilhelm Altmann's extensive *Handbuch für Streichquartettspieler* of 1927. Corresponding to its more practical aim, that work emphasized concise characterizations of the individual works rather than historical connections and analytic details. It gives brief summaries in a dictionary-like, pedagogical way — scarcely statements that set forth at least a part of the history of this genre, a good 230 years old today. On the contrary, the detailed monographic study, philological or analytical, has not progressed further since Wilhelm Altmann. The most striking example is the "unmasking" of Roman Hofstetter as the author of Haydn's op. 3. Less spectacular but musicologically just as important are the numerous quartet analyses and investigations from many countries, the results of which have nevertheless been absorbed only slowly and partially into either professional and amateur musical practice or popular musical literature, which in recent years has found increasing interest and wider dissemination. The present volume seeks to redress this deficiency in one area, discussing the first golden age of the string quartet from its beginnings around 1750 up to the death of Beethoven in 1827 and Schubert in 1828. The cutoff point at around 1830 has been placed at the creative end of the last two composers of the Viennese classic era, but this also has an esthetic, general and historical basis. The development of quartet style after

1830 takes another path, operating under other presuppositions and requiring another manner of performance on which the author is now at work.

The contents of the present work on the first eighty years of a new genre — necessarily selected, concentrated and compressed in the manner of a verbal summary — fall into an area between scientific precision, accuracy and correctness of detail on the one hand, and a more informal style, free of scientific jargon, on the other. The author does not believe that a written presentation of artistic facts must renounce all freedom, fantasy and metaphorical description, as long as the writer is aware that he is pursuing a fundamentally unattainable goal, and of the dangers that lie therein. The concentration on the quartet production of a few composers between 1750 and 1830 and the decision not to present lesser masters and their works is in keeping with the aims of this book. No matter how musicologically interesting the presentation of one or another development, no matter how pressing the case for one or another wrongfully neglected work might be, the scope of this book demands that it must be foregone in favor of the comprehensive, total picture.

In content, this volume breaks fresh musicological ground only in details, and many times takes its direction from the results of critical studies. Nevertheless the author is accountable for any emphasis, stress, or ascribed judgment. The basic literature is cited in the notes and bibliography. Above all, special thanks are due Professor Ludwig Finscher of Frankfurt, who gave the author many detailed references, and who was also so good as to read over critically every chapter upon completion.

Nuremberg, July 1979   Wulf Konold

Introduction

"A string quartet is, in the widest sense, any composition for four solo string instruments. In a narrower sense, it is a multi-movement work for two violins, a viola and cello."[1] The first is an intentionally formal definition of a musical genre that is often viewed today as the most demanding form of chamber music, of instrumental music, even of all western music, and it carries with it some general presuppositions. But the position that this genre has unanimously held since the second third of the nineteenth century in the view of composers, performers, public and music theorists is not, nor can it be, accounted for by such express assumptions. This estimation of value is connected with, but not congruent to, the genre's development and its outstanding examples. There are, in addition, some tendencies which in part reach further back historically, and others that are less explicitly musical and more of a general esthetic character, in which sociological realities play a role. In this brief introduction, which of course cannot comprehend a detailed presentation of a genre theory,[2]

---

1   Quoted from Ludwig Finscher, "Streichquartett" in *MGG*, vol 12, col 1559. Historical information concerning the theory of the string quartet in particular, as well as numerous contemporary sources are found in Ludwig Finscher, *Studien zur Geschichte des Streichquartetts* I (Kassel, 1974), 277ff.

2   Apart from the important groundbreaking work of Ludwig Finscher, a well-rounded theory of the string quartet, documented by sources, is at this time still a goal of musicology.

the basis for this high esteem can only be suggested. Technical prerequisite for the string quartet, and older than it by far, is the principle of four voice composition, considered perfect and complete since the sixteenth century, especially in vocal music. Four voice composition (the emancipation from three voice texture as a model already signified an impulse of musical secularization), was esteemed as highly by Palestrina, Lassus and Monteverdi as by Bach, and it increasingly took on the elements of regular compositional principles. In it was seen, above all, a musical medium combining intimacy, immediacy and introspection along with individualization of each voice and detail-conscious structural complexity. Four voice composition, in which good composers sharpened their skills, made common errors readily obvious, and corresponds to the four human voice types of soprano, alto, tenor and bass. By renouncing outward brilliance it allows not only compositional concentration on a narrow range, but above all has a flair for intimacy and, in its ideal state, unity of performer and listener, the latter naturally an open-minded connoisseur. Four voice composition (and, in this tradition, the string quartet) therefore also has an esthetic existence apart from all outward adornment; a form in which the concept of "more than meets the eye" was valid almost up to the present day. The metaphorical comparisons used by those holding an enlightened view of music in the late eighteenth century and early nineteenth centuries point up another side of the "veneration". Already in Mattheson, Scheibe, J. A. Schulz and Schubart one finds what Goethe formulated in one well known statement. When he heard a string quartet, Goethe reported, he had the impression that he "heard four rational people conversing with one another." The concept of discourse took its place from then on in the theory of the genre. In addition there is a reduction to four largely homogeneous sounding instruments, evolving independently within the fully formed genre, having broken out of the "eggshell of the basso continuo," showing a tonal and coloristic frugality and modesty that corresponded with those puristic elements of rationalism, ever more dominant during the eighteenth century. The supposed deficiency of the string quartet in the face of the colorfulness of the tonally evolving orchestra was turned into a virtue: the development of quartet style through Beethoven, Brahms and Schoenberg was founded on structural principles, on the science of composition, on the elaboration of various combinatorial possibilities in theme, motive, voice leading and counterpoint. This evolutionary line dominated in theory as well as in appreciation in preference to a deviating line in which coloristic principles played a predominant — and structurally defined — role. How much this structural evolutionary line dominated is perhaps shown by the generally low rank of wind quartets and string trios: such works — even those by Mozart — bear the indelible mark of the bastard.

The second important element contributing to the exalted rank of the string quartet was an act of very canonization. From their first appearances, Haydn's op. 33 string quartets and Mozart's six "Haydn" quartets based on them were valued not only as creative masterpieces but also as exemplary models of the new genre. The genre theory formulated in the nineteenth century always looked back in reverence to the stature of these works, while the late quartets of Beethoven long continued to seem strange. This genre theory along with its theses — either formulated or handed on in compositional *communis opinio* — extended largely unchallenged over the musical development of a good 200 years, through a social structure changing from the narrow courtly circle of the performing dilettantes, through the *Kenner und Liebhaber,* and into the professionalization of performers in the 1820's. What separates the string quartet from all other instrumental genres, including the symphony, is its displacement from intimate, private chambers into the ever more anonymous performance arena of the concert hall, and finally its wide dissemination through the technical media of our century. Within the compositional canon the works of a Schoenberg, a Bartók, a Webern adhere to the same principles and make the same demands as Haydn's quartets and, after a few iconoclastic power moves, it appears that at least in matters of structural complexity and cohesiveness the old tradition is still valid for today's most prized quartets.

The Beginnings

Certain musical forms are comparatively easily identified, with each new step forward theoretically postulated and practically carried out. All this may be so clear (as is perhaps the case with opera) that one need not consider matters of priority. The situation is quite different with the string quartet. Here we have an ongoing discussion[1] over when the genre began, and the opposing arguments are nourished by the variety of criteria considered necessary to the genre. Mere four voice texture ought not to suffice, since then the beginnings of the symphony, quartet and overture would coincide. But if one assumes that the string quartet proceeded step by step from a series of different older genres and if one sets down, as has Ludwig Finscher,[2] a fundamental group of criteria toward a defi-

1 See Edward J. Dent, "The earliest string quartets," *Monthly Musical Record* 33 (1903); Hugo Riemann, "Mannheimer Kammermusik des 18. Jahrhunderts," introduction to DTB *XV* (Leipzig, 1914); Fausto Torrefranca, "La lotta par l'egemonia musicale nel settecento, *RMI* 24 (1917) and 25 (1918); Torrefranca, "Le origini dello stilo mozartiano," *RMI* 28 (1921); Torrefranca, "Avviamento alla storia del quartetto italiano" *L'Approdo Musicale* 23 (1966); Marc Pincherle, "On the origins of the string quartet," *MQ* 15 (1929); A. Eaglefield Hull, "The earliest known string quartet," *MQ* 15 (1929); Hugo Rothweiler, "Zur Entwicklung des Streichquartets im Rahmen der Kammermusik des 18. Jahrhunderts" (diss., Tübingen, 1934; typescript); P. Schlüter, *Die Anfänge des modernen Streichquartetts* (Bleicherode, 1939).

2 Ludwig Finscher, *Studien zur Geschichte des Streichquartetts* I (Kassel, 1974), *Saarbrücker Studien zur Musikwissenschaft* 3; also Ursula Lehfmann, *Deutsches und italienisches Wesen in der Vorgeschichte des Klassischen Streichquartetts* (Würzburg, 1939).

nition, there can be pointed out in the late seventeenth and first half of the eighteenth century stylistic, technical and regionally varied developments that have all contributed to the string quartet's development without directly leading to it. The material at our disposal today admits of the conclusion that there were indeed many forerunners, but that the origin of the string quartet must have been the 'invention,' the compositional discovery, of two composers experimenting independently: Joseph Haydn and Luigi Boccherini.

The various preliminary stages that contributed toward the creation of the new genre can be arranged geographically, historically and stylistically. There were developments in Italy, France and Germany in the concerto, symphony and ensemble sonata all in connection with the emancipation of composition from the basso continuo, and from *obligato* style. All these contributed to the development of a genre-specific style, which led in turn to the evolution of the string quartet.

Italy in the late seventeenth and early eighteenth century was the land of opera. Except for an exclusive circle in Venice, Milan and Padua, instrumental music was scarcely cultivated. Composers like Antonio Vivaldi, Francesco Geminiani, Giuseppe Tartini and Giovanni Battista Sammartini were outsiders, more esteemed in the circle of the courtly and upper class civic *Kenner und Liebhaber* than by the general public. Proof of this borderline existence is the fact that most instrumental works of Italian provenance were printed in France, if at all. And a versatile instrumental composer like Luigi Boccherini was first appreciated only when he was active in France and Spain.

It was different in France, or, more accurately for that time, in Paris. Instrumental music received high public acclaim (especially since the founding of the *concerts spirituel* in 1725) and was cultivated in house concerts and by private orchestras. This appreciation goes back to the rich tradition of instrumental music at the French court since Lully and Rameau, and also to the fact that for a long time cultured people had considered the French language unsuitable for opera because of its complicated prosody. In the eighteenth century Paris had a fully developed musical life dependent on the influx of foreign music and musicians, and in which music publishing particularly flourished. Up to about 1740 Italian music was the dominant influence; thereafter the new south German and Bohemian school, the so called "Mannheim" style, held sway.

This development took a different course in German and Austrian lands. Here there was no public concert life as in France and, soon, in England.[3] Chamber music was carried on among the nobility, in the cloister, and especially by the civic *collegia musica*, founded around the turn of the century (many of them by Georg Philipp Telemann) in Leipzig, Frankfurt and Augsburg.

Historical roots of the string quartet are found in the *sinfonia a quattro*, in which the fourth voice — in Italy the viola and in France the third violin — still proceeded mostly in octaves with the bass, a heritage of the old trio sonata. Ritornello-like alternation between solo and tutti and the dominant basso continuo texture assign this sinfonia (not stylistically separable from the opera and concert sinfonia) to the "age of the basso continuo" as it was called by Hugo Riemann.[4] The *sonata a quattro*

3 Concerning the public concert see Heinrich W. Schwab, *Konzert* (Leipzig, 1971), *Musikgeschichte in Bildern* IV, 2, esp. 8f. and 19; Walter Salmen, *Haus- und Kammermusik* (Leipzig, 1969), *Musikgeschichte in Bildern* IV, 3, 18ff., 31ff.

4 Hugo Riemann, *Geschichte der Musiktheorie* (Berlin, 1898); books 1 and 2 trans. by Raymond H. Haggh (Lincoln, Neb., 1962), book 3 trans. by William C. Mickelson (Lincoln, Neb., c. 1977).

should be seen as a preliminary development, and not, as one often reads,[5] as a string quartet *per se*; it is at bottom only an enlarged trio sonata, or indeed an expanded *sonata da chiesa* in strict style. Alessandro Scarlatti's *Sei sonate a quattro senza cembalo* of around 1716 can do without the basso continuo since they are polyphonic throughout. They are, however, not string quartets. The *concerto a quattro*, a chamber music form of concerted sonata — as examples by Giuseppe Torelli and Antonio Vivaldi show — is also only one milestone, albeit an important one, in the development. From it there arose in the second half of the eighteenth century the specifically French-Italian type of *quatuor concertant*.[6]

The south German *Quartettsinfonie* and the *Quartett-divertimento*, often shortened in its own day to "string quartet," likewise represents merely a preliminary stage. The *Quartettsinfonie* is found from the beginning of the eighteenth century among the works of Frantisek Tuma and Georg Matthias Monn and, like the *sonata a quattro*, is a further development of the *sonata da chiesa*, a regular polyphonic form still valued at the beginning of the nineteenth century as a classic example of the strict sacred style. Wolfgang Amadeus Mozart and Ludwig van Beethoven were practiced in this manner of writing, the former in his church sonatas and the latter in his early preludes and fugues for string quartet. After the *Quartettsinfonie*, the rather popular, folky divertimento dominated in southern Germany, Austria and Bohemia. At the same time theory-bound, conservative north Germany kept to the

5 According to Fausto Torrefranca, *op. cit.*

6 On this matter see also Giuseppe Roncaglia, "Di G. G. Cambini, quartettista padre," *Rass. Mus.* 4 (1933); Dieter Lutz Trimpert, *Die Quatuor concertants von Giuseppe Cambini* (Tutzing, 1967).

rules of strict composition and dependence on the basso continuo into the 1780's. The *Quadri* originating there — for example by Georg Philipp Telemann — are mostly in a mixed style and go back to the example of the trio sonata.

Besides these historical prerequisites there were general stylistic and esthetic changes that influenced the development of the string quartet, first of all liberation from the basso continuo. The end of this bass function and a start toward homogeneity of the overall sound — interdependent elements of compositional technique — are noticeable from the beginning of the eighteenth century.[7] On the other hand there were up to 1783 still editions of Haydn's quartets in which the cello part was provided with basso continuo figures.

Into the same time period fall the stylistic distinction of tutti and solo playing and their anchoring in texture and structure, as well as the disuse of the improvisatory practice still in existence in other areas. Thus one should not be deceived by the name "chamber sonata," a much older conception of "chamber music."[8] "Chamber" in the eighteenth century referred to the performance and social setting of a work and did not have the present day meaning of one player to a part.

There is still one stylistic element to be considered: the development of a tonally homogeneous four voice instrumental texture. The structural development of the violin family as well as the changing esthetic and theoretical view of this type of composition were coequal prerequi-

7 Fritz Oberdörffer, *Der Generalbaß in der Instrumentalmusik des ausgehenden 18. Jahrhunderts* (Kassel, 1939).

8 See Fritz Salmen, *loc. cit.*, 10; Homer Ulrich, *Chamber music* (2nd ed., New York, 1966), 2ff.

sites. Clear definition of range and idiomatic characteristics contributed to the development of a violin capable of soloistic and virtuoso tasks.[9] Its new family eventually crowded out the dominant type of gamba ensemble used in the seventeenth century, especially in England. The contemporaneous existence of gamba and cello is illustrated most clearly in the works of J. S. Bach: within a short space of time he wrote solo suites for the full toned, virtuosic cello and sonatas for the gamba, the timbre of which blends well with cembalo.

This cursory enumeration of stylistic and historical elements makes it clear that the string quartet's evolution is built on an abundance of elements, no single one of which led directly to the new genre. Ludwig Finscher hit the mark when he wrote: "As it took shape among the classical models in the works of Haydn and Mozart (and in its theory largely derived from these works) the concept of string quartet combined many different elements of earlier genres as well as contemporary formal and stylistic concepts, creating in itself a new unity. In this new unity are met the following: four voice texture and the homogeneous sound of a solo ensemble of instruments from the same string family; the differentiation of these textures and sounds in filigree work, obligato accompaniment and, in the ideal, equality of the four voices; the cyclic sonata form in its various manifestations; the classical canon of apparent simplicity created from varied multi-layered compositional forms and the principle of thematic/motivic work; and the language of chamber music with its aura of intense introversion and subtle intimacy."[10]

9 On this subject see Walter Kolneder, *Das Buch von der Violine* (Zurich, 1972); Alberto Bachmann, *The encyclopedia of the violin* (New York, 1966), 1ff., 158ff., 166ff.

10 Finscher, *loc. cit.*, 16.

Joseph Haydn

"The central importance of Haydn for the development of that type of string quartet commonly called classical (not only in the sense of its defining an era, but also in the sense of its perfect unfolding and harmonic organization of all the possibilities immanent in the genre) was already recognized in Haydn's lifetime. Since Haydn's death his importance has been considered epochal, and has been described and interpreted with increased historical understanding and discrimination."[1] Among experts and musicologists the appreciation of Haydn unfortunately remains, to this day, inversely proportional to his importance in musical culture. The popular concept of "Papa Haydn" still looms large, and Robert Schumann's Romantic condemnation appears meaningful yet: "One hears nothing new from him. He is like a familiar houseguest, always

---

[1] Ludwig Finscher, *Studien zur Geschichte des Streichquartetts I. Die Entstehung des klassischen Streichquartets. Von den Vorformen zur Grundlegung durch Joseph Haydn.* (Kassel, 1974), 129. *Saarbrücker Studien zur Musikwissenschaft,* 3.

The Haydn chapter of the present work is indebted in many details to the work of Ludwig Finscher. In addition, the following basic works must also be mentioned: Adolf Sandberger, "Zur Geschichte des Haydn'schen Streichquartetts," *Altbayr. Monatsschrift* 2 (1900) and in *idem., Ausgewählte Aufsätze,* vol. 1 (Munich, 1921); Friedrich Blume, "Haydns künstlerische Persönlichkeit in seinen Streichquartetten," *Jahrbuch Peters* 37 (1931), and in *idem, Syntagma musicologicum,* vol. 1 (Kassel, 1963), 526ff.; Reginald Barrett-Ayres, *Haydn and the string quartet* (London, 1974); but see also the reviews of Finscher by Georg Feder in *Mf* 29 (1976), 106, and by James Webster in *JAMS* (1977), for correction of details and on other matters.

well and respectfully received, but he holds no deeper interest for the present day." In the development of the string quartet, however, Haydn's role should not be underestimated, and his influence reaches up to Arnold Schoenberg. The more than sixty string quartets proven to be by Haydn[2] originated over a period of almost half a century, between 1755 and 1803. In a recent investigation of the chronology of Haydn's quartets, American musicologist James Webster came to the following order:[3]

opp. 1 and 2	1755–1759	opp. 54 and 55	1788
op. 9	1769/70	op. 64	1790
op. 17	1771	opp. 71 and 74	1793
op. 20	1772	op. 76	1797
op. 33	1781	op. 77	1799
op. 42	1784/85	op. 103	1802
op. 50	1787		

As Ludwig Finscher has shown in great detail,[4] Haydn's first compositions for string quartet are based on the south German and Austrian divertimento. Boccherini's first printed string quartets show mature technique and qualities specific to the genre, but with Haydn it is the consistency in the development of the string quartet concept, and the thoroughly experimental broadening of the tonal and structural boundaries that define the evolution up to op. 33 and through the following quartet cycles. Haydn's biographer Georg August Griesinger has described the origin of the first quartets:

2 See H. C. Robbins Landon, "Doubtful and spurious quartets and quintets attributed to Haydn," *MR* 18 (1957), and Anthony von Hoboken, *Joseph Haydn. Thematisch-bibliographisches Werkverzeichnis*, vol. 1 (Mainz, 1957).

3 James Webster, "The chronology of Haydn's string quartets," *MQ* 61 (1975), 17–46, esp. 44.

4 Finscher, *loc. cit.*, 137–165.

"... the following quite casual circumstance caused him to try his hand at quartet composition. A Baron Fürnberg had a residence in Weinzierl, a few post-coach stops from Vienna, and from time to time he invited his pastor, his estate steward, Haydn and Albrechtsberger (a cellist and brother of the well-known contrapuntist) in order to hear a little music. Fürnberg asked Haydn to compose something that could be performed by these four musical companions."[5]

Griesinger's account is informative in more than one way: he not only gives the exact occasion for the composition of the first quartets, but describes the social situation for which string quartets were composed, both then and up to the beginning of the nineteenth century, especially in southern Germany and Austria. "In the eighteenth century, the palaces and gardens of the ruling aristocracy became exquisite homes of chamber music. Here music was made by servants as well as by the nobility itself — a most noble pastime carried on as *conversation galante et amusante* and *requisit eines galant-homme*. Here, and often with expert enthusiasm, music flourished in the best conditions."[6]

Haydn's quartets op. 1 and 2, which arose in this connection, are "in every detail small-scaled and loosely constructed, technically and musically rather unpretentious works. Stylistically they are well in the sphere of the divertimento and take up elements of various traditions, not contrasting them experimentally but naively juxtaposing them."[7] All twelve quartets of these two cycles

5 Georg August Griesinger, *Biographische Notizen über Joseph Haydn* (Leipzig, 1810), 12f.

6 Walter Salmen, *Haus- und Kammermusik* (Leipzig, 1969), 19. *Musikgeschichte in Bildern*, IV, 3.

7 Finscher, *loc. cit.*, 138.

are in five movements, with two very fast outer movements, a very slow middle movement and two minuets, all in the same key. There was very little of a quartet idiom in the writing of these early works; in fact the B♭ major quartet op. 7 no. 5 was originally a symphony.[8] It was probably first reworked as a quartet by the publisher in order to fill out the usual number of six works in a cycle. In addition the C major quartet op. 1 no. 6 was possibly originally a lute trio, made into a quartet by the composer.

The shape and structure of these early works can be illustrated by example of B♭ major quartet op. 1 no. 1. The first movement, with its *presto* tempo, key, and 6/8 meter, is a divertimento-like "caccia" movement. Unisons, themes made up of broken triads, conversational interplay between upper and lower voices, and finally virtuoso emphasis on the upper voice are all formal elements quite at home in popular music. Although the first movement is in sonata form (exposition: m. 1-24; development: m. 25-40; recapitulation: m. 41-62), the technical structure barely shows clear three part form and regular harmonic framework. No contrasting theme is used. The voice leading is clearly paired and the viola part runs parallel with the cello almost throughout. Dynamic contrast and sequential dialogue technique serve for musical variety.

8 Finscher, *loc. cit.*, 140; and H. C. Robbins Landon, *The symphonies of Joseph Haydn* (London, 1955), supplement.

Example 1

Presto

The minuets (second and fourth movements of the work) are likewise in the courtly *galant* style. The first is clearly homophonic, with the emphasis on the upper voice, and tonally (E♭ major) and technically (dialogue style) contrasting trio. The second minuet works with motivic imitation between the upper and lower voices and has a simple homophonic trio. The slow movement (*adagio*) is a highly ornamented showpiece for the first violin with an accompaniment pattern of repeated sixteenths. Only its expressive introduction, which presents the key of E major and returns at the end, appears technically demanding in its chorale-like vocal texture.

The last movement, a B$^\flat$ major *presto* in 2/4, is so like the opening movement in shape and structure that the two movements seem interchangeable (as is the case throughout op. 1). "Thematic contrast, as well as motivic reduction and elaboration, grow from dialogue technique and *Fortspinnung* melodies. This is all still on the smallest scale, but accomplished with a compositional logic that takes in nothing less than a thorough consideration of all possibilities presented in these very same dialogue and *Fortspinnung* techniques."[9]

Haydn's op. 2, based on the same model in the order of its movements, presents on the contrary a step forward towards conscious shaping of the genre in the greater importance of individual movements as well as stylistic and formal unity, a clear contrast to the colorful mix of op. 1. This tendency is especially apparent in the structure of the first movements. While in op. 1 first and last movements were of the same virtuoso-popular type, the first movements of op. 2 are weightier, slower in tempo, expanded in structure, and more technically demanding, while the last movements retain their dance-finale character. Minuets and slow movements on the other hand stay in the same musical sphere as op. 1. In the step from op. 1 to op. 2, Haydn's systematic formation and differentiation of the individual movement types and characters are al-

9 Finscher, *loc. cit.*, 146.

ready apparent. By op. 33 this leads to the classical four movements clearly distinguished from one another by compositional emphases and formulations. There is often mentioned a gap of a good ten years between op. 20 and op. 33, during which time no string quartets were written. But this same chronological situation exists between op. 2 and op. 9. (The controversial op. 3 is doubtless not by Haydn but rather is proven to be by Roman Hofstetter and can therefore be left out of this discussion.[10]) The gap between op. 2 and op. 9, first of all, has a biographical basis. Since 1761 Haydn was vice-*Kapellmeister* at Esterhazy and the greater part of his creative output lay in those forms used at court, namely the symphony and the baryton trio. Therefore the experimental testing of new techniques specific to chamber music was carried out in the 1760's in the baryton trio.[11]

The op. 1 and 2 string quartets originated within five years of each other. They appeared somewhat out of sequence, were initiated through a casual form of music making, and were first put together in cycles by the publisher. The following quarters, however, present quite another picture. Within just three years, between 1770 and 1772, there came a total of eighteen quartets that were put together as three cycles by the composer himself. Among the technical elements which unify the op. 9, 17 and 20 cycles (despite all their differences) are: "vocal quality of the part writing and the polyphonic enrichment of the harmony, the equalization of concertant elements

10 See Alan Tyson and H. C. Robbins Landon, "Who composed Haydn's op. 3?" *Musical Times* 195 (1964), 506f.; Laszlo Somfai, "Zur Echtheitsfrage des Haydn'schen op. 3," *Haydn Yearbook* 3 (1965), 153–165; Hubert Unverricht, *Die beiden Hoffstetter. Zwei Komponistenporträts mit Werkverzeichnissen* (Mainz, 1968); summary in Finscher, *loc. cit.*, 168–190.

11 Concerning this see Finscher, *loc. cit.*, 160ff.

and motivic work, the broadening and concentrated over-all structuring of the forms, the distinct individualization of the character of each movement, interconnection of the movements (making a cyclic form out of an accepted order of movements), intentional 'composition' of a whole opus from six pieces not casually thrown together but fitting with and complementing each other."[12] The decision of the aged Haydn to begin a planned complete edition of his string quartets with op. 9 shows that with it came a compositional new beginning on a higher plane, on the level of a specific genre style. "... I was cut off from the world. No one in my vicinity could confuse or pester me, and so I was forced to be original."[13] Haydn's statement, transmitted by Griesinger, finds its first expression in these quartets, in a detailed evolutionary process owing almost nothing to outside influences, which fixed the new compositional form with its systematic formal control and characterizations. Here Haydn continued slowing the first movement tempo, a process already introduced in op. 2. The op. 9 and 17 quartets show a *cantabile moderato* type, and a lack of thematic contrast is compensated for by the permeation of the whole work with motivic elaboration. The sonata-allegro form, with exposition, development and recapitulation, theoretically restricted all thematic work solely to the development, a restriction gradually overcome in the music of the second half of the eighteenth century. Here the strict, pedantic scheme is given up in favor of continual "development." For example, the first movement of the C major quartet op. 9 no. 1 leads, after a few measures, to a contrapuntal independence of the voices,

12 Finscher, *loc. cit.*, 193.

13 Griesinger, *loc. cit.*, 17.

with melodic elements taken from the motives of the main theme, here set singly against one another (m. 15-18):

Example 2

The recapitulation is no longer an exact recall; its entrance is disguised, its course is altered and it is abbreviated. It functions as a reactive response to the development. The overall ternary character of the early sonata-allegro form here gives way to a thoroughgoing developmental form, constructed of single elements, their variations and conjunctions. From op. 9 Haydn used a four movement scheme, with only the position of the minuet varying in the order of the movements. These minuets lost their "ballroom" character, became more reserved, shed that pleasantly agreeable melodic style and, on the contrary, became more demanding in their technical refinements. There is especially noticeable a metrical irregularity, which forever after avoided symmetries of equal numbers of measures, and which often joined sections of different lengths. With developmental elements finding their way into the dance movement, it began an evolution from *Charakterstück* to scherzo.[14] The slow movements on the other hand are still closely bound to tradition. Here Haydn could look back to and adapt a number of traditional forms, from the aria to the trio sonata and concerto. An expansion of the existing material in matters of detail and an escape from rigid formal principles are also found here. This is most impressive perhaps in the *szene* for violin and accompanying parts in the E^b major quartet op. 9 no. 2, in which Haydn combines recitative and arioso elements into a virtuoso "musical discussion" in the esthetic sense of the eighteenth century, thereby overriding strict formal sectionalization.

Finally, last movements retain their *presto-capriccio* character: terse structure, expressly virtuso texture for all

14 Concerning the investigation of compositional types among Haydn's minuets and scherzi in the symphony and string quartets see Wolfram Steinbeck, *Das Menuett in der Instrumentalmusik Joseph Haydns* (Munich, 1973).

four instruments with the upper voice clearly dominating, and, now and then, the use of folky elements. In the finale of op. 9 no. 3 Haydn quotes the folksong "Die Katz, die läßt das Mausen nicht," which also appears in Mozart's Divertimento KV 252 and in Beethoven's piano concerto op. 15. But there are also some tendencies toward contrapuntal-fugal structure, as in the finale of op. 9 no. 4. The collection of six works into a clearly unified "opus" is shown in the key succession (op. 9: no. 1 in C major, no. 2 in E major, no. 3 in G major, no. 4 in d minor, no. 5 in B major, no. 6 in A major) with its preference for the upper portion of the circle of fifths. There is also, however, an internal structural ordering to the quartets, one which Haydn retained up to op. 76 (and on which basis the half-cycles of op. 54 and 55, and op. 71 and 74 can be put together). In this ordering, each cycle of six quartets contains at least one quartet in minor, and the quartets at the end of the cycle are always looser in structure and more concertant-popular. The first quartets of cycles, on the other hand, are usually technically most demanding. This ordering is already apparent in op. 9. In op. 9 no. 5 an introductory sonata movement is replaced by a slow variation movement, and the very fast (*presto*) and flashy first movement of op. 9 no. 6, (corresponding to Haydn's typical use of A major) is planned more for specifically violinistic virtuosity than motivic-thematic concentration.

"The four movement string quartet type of op. 9 appears after all as an exceedingly complex structure. In it are blended old and new, strange and familiar, rudiments of the quartet divertimento and elements reaching far into the future, the musical idiom of C. P. E. Bach and the logic of Haydn's formal development, striving for expression

15 Cf. references in Finscher, *loc. cit.*, 204, and appendix, 386–387.

and individualization of traditional movements and formal types. And all this is ruled by an intellectual pretension and an intensified rationality of compositional work, for which there is nothing comparable either in Haydn's symphonies of these years or in his baryton trios."[16]

The six op. 17 quartets (no. 1 in E major, no. 2 in F major, no. 3 in E♭ major, no, 4 in e minor, no. 5 in G major, no. 6 in D major) continue the line of development begun in op. 9. The minuets still are second movements here, and document the progressive path of emancipation from dance minuet to character piece. The minuet of op. 17 no. 1, for example, shows a two part thematic structure with dynamic and melodic contrast. The occasional opposition of contrapuntal and homophonic textures underscores this character contrast. The slow movements exhibit a multiplicity of formal types including the 'scene' in op. 17 no. 5 (encompassing aria and recitative), the clearly sectionalized *Siciliano* type in op. 17 no. 1, and the A♭ major *adagio* in the style of C. P. E. Bach in op. 17 no. 3. But it is the harmonic enrichment and the achievement of a full overall sound specific to the new genre that separates this cycle from the more treble-dominated slow movements of op. 9. Virtuosity and concertant looseness are the chief formal elements of the last movements. The first movements, again mostly in gentle *moderato* tempi, still concentrate on variants of thematic unity. Op. 17 no. 3 begins, as does op. 9 no. 5, with a variation movement, while op. 17 no. 6 has the oft used *chasse* character. Instead of regular thematic contrast, different forms of the theme take on the function of main, secondary and closing themes all being developed out of one motive. The recapitulation, its entry obscured, is shortened and, now and

16 Finscher, *loc. cit.*, 205.

bond which is also found in structural principles: asymmetrical phrasing, offbeat melodic forms, isolation of a trill motive as a germ cell of the thematic elaboration and, finally, in the melodic identity of the openings of minuet and finale.

Example 3

The slow movement stands quite apart from all this, self-contained by virtue of its thematic independence, contrasted by the key of G major, combining thematic work and concertant soloistic elements. The first movement, with its quick *allegro con sprito* 2/4 meter, abandons the *moderato* tempo of the first movements of op. 17 and takes on something of the *finale* flavor without taking over its precise tone. It is characterized by thick successions of accents, asymmetric seven measure shape of the theme, expressive chromaticism quickly alternating with melodic leaps. The contrasting thematic material, already developed in the first measures, is constructed from motivic elements of the main theme. Structure and stability are achieved in this thematically fragmented movement through emphasized organ points and the inclusion of an instrumental pathos usually reserved to the symphony. The development builds up the thematic fragmention to the point where constructive concentration is transformed into immediate expressivity. "The crucial spot in this development is the third section, where unresolved conflict between head and contrasting motives turns the technique of motivic reduction into an expressive dramatic event which (. . .) holds a decisive new meaning: what could be understood in the exposition as an interplay of musical contrast (. . .), using the predetermined forms of dramatic music, now seizes the elements of the movement itself as the substance of a dramatic conflict."[20]

Example 4

M. 141

20 Finscher, *loc. cit.*, 224.

34

The recapitulation is subject to the radical consequences of this conflict. It is much abbreviated with further developmental elements intercalated, and a developmental coda added.

While the form of the first movement threatens to disintegrate under the assault of constructive miniaturization and dramatic expression, two evolutionary lines cross in the minuet. "The tendency of the earlier quartets toward extreme logical consistency is still found, but a path to the classical minuet is already being broken here."[21] The g minor minuet illustrates this opposition between minuet and trio: tendencies of the lyrical character piece and stylized *Ländler* mark both lines of development. The last movement is in an obligato three voice texture but eventually proves to be a compactly worked out sonata allegro movement. It is not as serious in tone as the first movement, though three other last movements of the cycle de-

21 *Ibid.*, 232.

velop into fugues. Nor is it as uncompromising in structure as the first movement: it declares itself a last movement through its terse layout. A well-developed independence of the voices can already be seen in the first measures.

Example 5

If the g minor quartet in its entirety is the most extreme of the whole cycle, as well as the most extreme Haydn quartet overall, we may also find further such characteristics in the single movements of the other quartets, especially in the last movements of the quartets in C major (op. 20 no. 2), f minor (op. 20 no. 5), and A major (op. 20 no. 6), in which Haydn, with considerable contrapuntal grandiloquence, writes multithematic fugues. If one uses Haydn's sketch catalog to order the quartets according to their origin, it appears that the three fugue quartets came first, and those with free contrapuntal and conventionally loose *finales* later, the conclusion then appears possible that already within this cycle the fugue *finale* seemed a dead end to Haydn. Moreover, if one examines the characteristics of the individual fugues this conclusion seems quite certain. Still, the fugues go from a traditional arrangement (in op. 20 no. 5) through individualized thematic forms (in op. 20 no. 6) a contrapuntal "character theme" type,[22] which no longer has anything in common with the Baroque *Schulfuge* and, indeed, so thoroughly integrates contrapuntal and sonata allegro elements that it effaces the "fugal" boundaries.

22 *Ibid.*

23 See Warren Kirkendale, *Fuge und Fugato in der Kammermusik des Rokoko und der Klassik* (Tutzing, 1966), 179—187.

Example 6

The above mentioned interpenetration of two principles
within the minuet is shown most clearly in the minuet of
the D major quartet op. 20 no. 4, where the designation
"alla Zingarese" and the simplicity of the symmetrical construction already indicate this new character and the influence of stylized folk music. This is, however, not a re-

turn to the "ballroom" minuet. The folk-musical sound melts away in the refined character of the string quartet, making this a stylistic derivation, not a copy.

"The overall impression of the op. 20 quartets seems (. . .) confusing mainly because it transects the various tendencies within it: stark differentiation of the movements' characters and the greatest possible unification of the cyclic form, opening of new areas of expression and layers of artistic formation in the absorption of folk musical elements into the minuet, a new technical dimension in increased motivic work and compositional craft, utmost formal rationalization in the g minor quartet, revolutionary expressivity of the 'conversational' ethos, the esthetic of a highly refined chamber music style and formal relations and rupture of the previous genre boundaries in the popular style of the dance minuet, in archaic tendencies and in symphonic pathos."[24]

After this expressive "boundary breaking" there is again a lapse of a scarce ten years in Haydn's quartet production. This time, however, the hiatus is not attributable to outside reasons but rather to the inner, technical problem of formulating a suitable reaction to the self-imposed demand of op. 20.

On December 3, 1781, Haydn wrote a subscription letter to a number of musical amateurs, offering them manuscript part copies of new string quartets before printing; in this letter Haydn makes the noteworthy statement that these works are "of an entirely new kind, since for the last ten years I have not written any at all."[25] Adolf Sandberger, Friedrich Blume and, in recent years, Ludwig Fin-

24 Finscher, *loc. cit.*, 236.

25 Collected in Georg Feder, "Ein vergessener Haydn-Brief," *Haydn-Studien* I/2 (1966), 114–116; likewise H. C. Robbins Landon and D. Bartha, *Joseph Haydn. Briefe und Aufzeichnungen* (Kassel, 1965).

scher,[26] have reached divergent conclusions from this which, if set forth here, would lead us too far afield. But Finscher's conclusion appears convincing: that this declaration is connected with a decisive new element in Haydn, the "art of often sounding familiar" as Ernst Ludwig Gerber put it;[27] and so there continues the tendency (already begun in the minuets of op. 20) of blending into the chamber musical organism something of the simple and familiar, thereby increasing its multiplicity of forms, and establishing a fundamental basis for the future, without trivializing the genre, or making it basely popular.

Aside from the part copies offered by Haydn in the spring of 1782, the six op. 33 string quartets (no. 1 in b minor, no. 2 in E$^\flat$ major, no. 3 in C major, no. 4 in B$^\flat$ major, no. 5 in G major, no. 6 in D major) were published concurrently by Artaria in Vienna and Hummel in Berlin. These works were highly praised by the *cognoscenti*,[28] and possess a formal modernization that Haydn had in the meantime developed in his symphonies, namely sonata-rondo form in the last movements, which now exhibit an interpenetration of the sequential rondo and the developmental sonata principles. Here, and not in the linking of fugue and sonata, lay the "classical" solution for Haydn. But this "entirely new style" can also be found by analysis in the other movements of these quartets: "the striving after simplicity and clarity is illustrated regularly

26 See note 1, Finscher, *loc. cit.*, 238ff.

27 Ernst Ludwig Gerber, *Historisch-biographisches Lexikon der Tonkünstler* (Leipzig, 1790), col. 610.

28 Cf., for example, the review by Johann Friedrich Reichardt in Musikalisches Kunst-Magazin 1782, col. 205, " . . . full of the most original caprices, and lively and most pleasing jokes. There has indeed never been a composer so full of originality and variety of expression combined with so much charm and popularity as Haydn, and few charming and popular composers have at the same time such good technique as Haydn has most of the time."

in the main themes of the sonata allegro movements. No longer does a single one of the six works begin with a polyphonic theme and obligato counterpoint. All the main themes, without regard to tempo and character, are conceived as songfully phrased and symmetrically grouped melodies with simple chordal accompaniment."[29]

Example 7

29 Finscher, *loc. cit.*, 246.

This melodizing of the thematic material does not mean, however, that Haydn had renounced the technical advances already achieved in the works since op. 20. This is evident in the first measures of the b minor quartet op. 33 no. 1. They are still used, but are subordinated to the compositional principle of clarity. Thus the analysis of the above-cited example from op. 33 no. 1 discloses a subtle kind of motivic reduction technique in passing the theme from first violin to cello, and in the melodizing of the chordal accompaniment in the second violin (m. 2). Nevertheless, the clear binary structure and songlike character of the theme are its dominant traits. "There is here the highest intensity of craft, an abundance of forms created through strong delineation of the material, simple clarity of form shaped by subtle refinement of details, dynamic formal growth in pulsating motion through the static, clearly articulated grouping, goal orientation of the development and regular back references, greatest variety in strictest unity."[30] All this makes up the "new style" of the sonata movements, and this principle applies to the other movement types as well. The last movements are unburdened of the weight they still bore in op. 20. Without giving up thematic elaboration they acquire a newly developed function and, as most notably in the E^b major quartet op. 33 no. 3, there is found in them what Reichardt apostrophized as the Haydnesque "humor" — not just a matter of a capricious theme or a clearly articulated detail, but rather a special "form-humor." Form here no longer simply means that which fulfills or — as in op. 20 — breaks a given mold, but instead indicates a self-evolving process, a "playful-form," whose fulfillment or surprising contravention, whose capricious unpredictability or play upon

30 *Ibid.*, 249.

anticipation makes up the "joke." This characteristic also appears in the scherzo-like minuets of op. 33, which include elements of the folky dance minuet as well as structural principles of sonata allegro movements. In their displaced symmetries, unanswered motivic statements and charming distortions of periodic eight measure structure they likewise show this new level of formal playfulness, as in the scherzo (Haydn calls the dance movements scherzi for the first time in op. 33) of op. 33 no. 5. After a four measure prelude with an emphasized caesura, there follows a section that opens chromatically, breaks off suddenly with a general pause — and then ends differently from what one is led to expect. The slow movements remain for the most part traditional — as shown in those of op. 33 no. 3 and no. 5. Here the upper voice still clearly dominates in an almost solo concerto-like texture. Meanwhile in op. 33 no. 2 and no. 4 the concertant principle of equalization of all four instruments is further developed.

"Haydn's op. 33 is the epochal work in which the string quartet found its first classical realization in the full meaning of the word (. . .); it is classical not only in the sense of a mature stylistic fulfillment, perceptible from the first *Quartett-divertimenti* on, but also in concrete musical details. It combines extreme clarity of form with a great capacity for variation of detail, basically homophonic texture with unfolding of the individual voices, subtle musical elaboration with seemingly simple musical effect, cyclic unity of overall form and character of the work with the unfolding of forms and characters of the individual movements."[32]

31 *Ibid.*, 256ff.; see also Willi Kahl, "Scherzo," *MGG*, vol. 11, col. 1684; Gustav Becking, *Studien zu Beethovens Personalstil. Das Scherzothema* (Leipzig, 1921), esp. 64—70.

32 Finscher, *loc. cit.*, 266.

Although these quartets are quite important for the history of the entire genre up to Beethoven's op. 59, the epochal position of Haydn's op. 33 within his own *œuvre* has generally been emphasized. Yet this should not lead to the misunderstanding that this "classical" form of string quartet composition remained unchanged from then on in Haydn's later quartets. Indeed there are found in his works up to 1802 no more such decisive developments, but Haydn did continue to experiment in matters of detail, questioning previously found solutions or examining them anew in a critical way. Six years lay between op. 33 and the next complete cycle, the op. 50 quartets dedicated to Frederick Wilhelm II,[33] king of Prussia, and in these six years only two more works appeared. The d minor quartet op. 42 belongs stylistically with op. 20, despite its relatively late date of origin (the sketch catalog indicates 1784/85). It begins with a slow sonata-allegro movement (*andante ed innocentemente*), the minuet comes second and the finale combines sonata principles with fugal structure. The op. 51 cycle is the string quartet version of the "seven words of Jesus Christ on the cross."[34] (There is also a keyboard setting.) This autograph reworking of the original orchestral score allows for interesting conclusions concerning the role of liturgical instrumental music. Yet within the genre of the string quartet it seems more a foreign object, with its introduction, seven slow movements and *presto* finale, "*Il Terremoto.*" This last, with its obvious programmatic effects, foreshadows the instrumental parts of Haydn's late oratorios.

33 Friedrich Wilhelm II, himself a practicing cellist, is also the dedicatee of Mozart's three last quartets KV 575, 589 and 590, and both cello sonatas op. 5 (1796) of Ludwig van Beethoven.

34 On the origin of this arrangement see Barrett-Ayres, *loc. cit.*, 178ff.

Haydn's op. 50 comprises six quartets (no. 1 in B♭ major, no. 2 in C major, no. 3 in E♭ major, no. 4 in f sharp minor, no. 5 in F major, no. 6 in D major) which follow the usual cyclic plan in key sequence, and in placement of the minor quartet and two rather lightweight works at the end. In the literature on op. 50[35] the thoroughgoing monothematicism is usually stressed. Development of thematic material from a single motivic cell, and lack of contrasting themes are features not only of the first movements, but of the minuets and finales as well. Apart from the fact that this technique (if not with such logical consistency) is already found in earlier quartets, this trait is still not the only characteristic element of this cycle. Along with this thematic concentration there runs through the entire course of a movement a ubiquitous developmental and motivic reduction technique, especially in the initial sonata movements, which has considerable consequences for the function of the recapitulation. Otherwise, as still happens in op. 20 and 33, Haydn does without a complete recapitulation in the first movements, instead usually presenting an almost exact recall of the main motives, as in op. 50 no. 1, with a second development section. To this is added a finely varied harmony, which in many places, through enharmonic reinterpretation and sudden shifts, reminds one of Schubert's harmonic style. Also startling are completely unconventional openings, such as that of the D major quartet op. 50 no. 6, which begins in the dominant, and reaches the tonic only in the fourth measure.

35 *Ibid.*, 202ff.

Example 8

In the minuets, now third movements throughout, thematic unity is likewise notable — a unity which goes so far
that the trios of op. 50 no. 4 and no. 5 are scarcely more
than minor variants of the minuet. The thematic concentration and the use of motivic reduction is so far-reaching
that the dance movement complex closely approaches a
true sonata-allegro movement. The last movements are also
monothematic, and are distinguished from the first movements by their terser structure, capricious tone and virtuosic instrumental layout. Yet they are sonata-allegro movements throughout and technically rest on the same principles as the first movements. Mixed forms somewhere between rondo and variations dominate the slow movements,
which are clearly set apart through monothematic connection to the other movements and through thematic correspondences between the slow movements themselves, as in
op. 50 no. 4 and no. 5. The most complex and contrary
is found in the *andante* of opus 50 no. 4 where a highly ex-

pressive dramatic style is produced by a five part variation-rondo form of two contrasting themes that, despite a sequential underlying structure, differ tonally (major-minor) and in character.

The op. 54, 55 and 64 quartets, written in the years 1788—1790, are also known as the "Tost" quartets, though it must be pointed out that only the printed edition of the op. 64 quartets bears the dedication to the Viennese merchant and former Esterhazy violinist. A few years earlier, Haydn had given the manuscripts of op. 54 and 55 for publication to Tost who was travelling to Paris. What Haydn experienced here is best described as an instance of what in the eighteenth century falls under the general heading of edition piracy.[36] The publication in two groups of three may also have had commercial rather than compositional grounds. The contemporaneous origin and — if one considers all the works together — the familiar tonal ordering (op. 54: no. 1 in G major, no. 2 in C major, no. 3 in E major; op. 55: no. 1 in A major, no. 2 in f minor, no. 3 in B^b major) also testify to their belonging together in one group. The testing of new techniques and combinations also continues in this cycle.[37] Concertant and symphonic elements are present and, in the last movements, various permutations of sonata-allegro, rondo and contrapuntal techniques play a dominant role. Monothematicism is given up — at least in the extreme degree found in op. 50: the sonata-allegro movements have clear second themes and codas. Yet within the development section these play a relatively small role, and in op. 54 no. 2 the second theme is only a brief lyric episode. Though the quartets op. 54

36 *Ibid.*, 228.

37 *Ibid.*, 230f.

and 55 are not dedicated to the violinist Tost, they are at least equal to his ability in their technical demands on the performer. Besides, Haydn may have been aiming for something like the *quatuor concertant* then popular in Paris in order to attract a new audience. But the virtuoso dominance of the first violin, expressed especially in its higher range, does not indicate a definite stylistic turn in the direction of the *quatuor brilliant*. It is mainly in the transitional sections that the violin is allowed to shine, and nowhere is the delicacy of the compositional technique or the fundamental equality of voices compromised.

Up to the f minor quartet op. 55 no. 2, which begins with an *andante piu tosto allegretto* variation movement followed by the sonata-allegro movement, the slow movements are in second place throughout. In them, Haydn intensifies the virtuoso-figurative play through harmonic variation, mostly derived from major-minor opposition. Only the *romance*-like *allegretto* of op. 54 no. 1 departs from this plan, being in a more popular style. The thematic connection between minuet and trio begun in op. 50 is developed further. In the C major quartet op. 54 no. 2 in particular, the trio is really only a thematic variant; moreover, melodic relationships to the main theme of the sonata movement point to cyclic planning. Orchestral elements, as in op. 54 no. 3, contrapuntal independence of voices, as in the double counterpoint texture of op. 55 no. 2, and finally the combination of dotted and triplet rhythm in op. 55 no. 3, which Schubert later developed into almost thematic significance — all these are elements that document Haydn's continuing concentration of work precisely in such apparently innocuous movements. The last movements also bear this out. In them the composer once again takes up the interplay of rondo and developmental principles, he builds in a clearly articulated varia-tion movement (in op. 54 no. 1) and fugal sections (in op. 55 no. 1 and 2). The contrapuntal condensation of thematic material and its combination with homophonic elements continues the line of development leading from the C major quartet op. 20 no. 2 to the f$^\sharp$ minor quartet op. 50 no. 4. This evolutionary line also differentiates Haydn's contrapuntal capriccio type more and more from his Baroque models, as well as from the quartet fugues of his contemporaries Albrechtsberger, Monn and Wagenseil, and from Mozart's fugue compositions.

The six op. 64 quartets written during the summer of 1790 mark an important turning point in the life of the composer, with his release from courtly service after the death of Prince Nicholas, and his first journey to England at the request of the impressario Johann Peter Salomon. Thus Haydn came into contact with that world for which he had been writing his quartets all along.

The op. 64 quartet cycle (no. 1 in C major, no. 2 in b minor, no. 3 in B$^\flat$ major, no. 4 in G major, no. 5 in D major, no. 6 in E$^\flat$ major) is also marked by Haydn's modern-experimental approach. Only the sonata-allegro movements show an abundance of new elements in their detail work:[38] specifically cyclic thematic unity, monothematic technique, the increasing inclusion of monothematic elements in the thematic work spanning the movements, and finally a har-monic expansion and emancipation of the coda, which in-creasingly took on the character of a second development section, rather than that of the cheery closing sweep. All these are elements that mark the first movements of this cycle. In addition there is greater spaciousness, with the

38 Cf. Barrett-Ayres, *loc. cit.*, 247ff, esp. 247–248.

movements' dimensions approaching the model of the contemporary symphonies no. 88 and 92, and there is also a
clearly virtuoso-concertant layout which, as in op. 54 and
55, certainly serves the thematic structure and, despite
the clear dominance of the first violin, engages the other
instruments in motivic work as well. Much like the distinction between Beethoven's op. 18 and op. 59, Haydn's op.
64 quartets clearly show that step by which Haydn led
away from the string quartet of the home music maker and
cultured amateurs to the concert quartet, whose refinements the knowledgeable listener could enjoy and whose
instrumental demands could generally be met only by professional musicians.

As always, Haydn continues to work with the sequence
of movements within a piece: both the minuets in op. 64
no 1 and no. 4 stand in second place, before a lively variation movement. When the slow movement has a solemn,
serious character the minuet is put before the finale, apparently with the function of separating the weightier and
lighter movements from each other. The tendency toward
sonata-form-like elaboration of the dance movement also
continues. The trios of op. 64 no. 1, 4 and 6 are thematic
variations of, or quite closely connected with their minuets,
but are generally contrasted by mode mixture.

The character of the last movements also varies within
the cycle and is definitely linked to the other movements
in any particular work. This, therefore, makes it clear that
Haydn depended more and more on an individual, unique
overall control to breathe life into a roughly schematized
formal outline: as a counterbalance to a first movement of
extensive proportions in op. 64 no. 1, he writes a highly
complex finale that combines the overall shape of a sonata form movement with extended contrapuntal and varia-

tion work in the development and recapitulation. The minuet and *allegretto* fairly pale in comparison with it. In op. 64 no. 2 on the other hand, there is a clear "lifting of the load" after the harmonically obscure, strongly chromatic first movement. This is achieved through the figurative and concertant elements in the *adagio*, which includes the remote key of B major and is largely in a bright, full sonority up to the virtuoso, monothematic last movement.

The B♭ major quartet op. 64 no. 3 perhaps shows the independence of the movements' individual characters most clearly. After a spacious concertant *vivace* there follows a three part *adagio* which ingeniously alters the model of the Baroque trio sonata (but achieves a distinctively romantic sound in the E♭ minor section). The finale, thematically related to the minuet and the first movement, is a type of sonata rondo. One more element takes on considerable importance in this cycle: in the slow movements especially, and in the minuet and trio pair, Haydn works increasingly with clearly contrasting color and range alterations, in part supporting harmonic contrasts but in part without emphasizing them, and instead opposing expressly 'light' and 'dark' sections to each other. The three part *adagio* of op. 64 no. 5 is almost entirely without these contrasts. While the finale of op. 64 no. 4 is predominantly characterized through its *chasse* character and its incorporation of sonata rondo elements, the finale of op. 64 no. 6 is set apart from the more songful first movement by the combination of rondo and fugal elements and its *perpetuum mobile* feeling — a new form of the Haydnesque 'capriccio.' In the E♭ major quartet, contrapuntal techniques play an important role, quite in contrast to the 'light' character of the other cycle closings. These techniques also characterize the *allegretto* first movement as well as the B♭ major *an-*

dante (where canon plays a large part) and the *presto* finale. In its symphonic layout as well as in the thematic relation of minuet and trio, the minuet here foreshadows that of the E^b major symphony no. 103.

Between the op. 64 quartets and those following (the op. 71 and 74 cycles which comprise only 3 quartets each) lay not only three years, but also the experience of the extended first visit to London. This experience left strong new impressions of the very different style of middle class concert life in the English capital and the effects of these impressions are realized in subsequent works. Although the op. 71 and 74 quartets are dedicated to Count Apponyi, residing in Pressburg, they address themselves to an anonymous middle class, concert-going public. The absorption of specifically symphonic elements; the use of an introduction to the first movement, whether a written out cadenza (as in op. 71 no. 1 and 3), a *coup d'archet,* or (as in op. 71 no. 2 and op. 74 no. 2 and 3) a fully formed slow introduction with thematic foreshadowings; the thematic 'unburdening' of the slow movement, in which more and more songful, romantic elements are found; and finally the instrumental virtuosity which, in the first movement of op. 71 no. 1, leaves room for a solo cadenza — all these point clearly to the changing social situation of the string quartet. Yet all this does not mean that the quartet had become 'superficial.' It now had, so to speak, two complementary levels: one large-scaled and brilliantly virtuosic, and the other structurally exacting. On these grounds, Mozart's statement pertaining to his piano concertos is applicable here: the quartets "... are very brilliant, pleasing to the ear — naturally never falling into emptiness. Connoisseurs can here and there derive all sorts of satisfaction, and yet the non-connoisseur will also be satisfied, without knowing why."

"Satisfaction for the connoisseur" is already shown in the B♭ major *Romanze* from op. 71 no. 3, whose theme and variations character Haydn very skillfully sets apart[39] through thematic relationship and concertant looseness. The minuets especially show symphonic elements and folk musical reminiscences in their unisons and echo effects; but melodic sighs, a certain dance character and metrical simplicity are also to be found.

In the three op. 74 quartets (no. 1 in C major, no. 2 in F major, no. 3 in g minor) Haydn succeeds particularly with a combination of refined detail work and quasi-symphonic openness, the capacity already described by Reichardt with regard to op. 33 of "often sounding familiar." Thus the first movement of op. 74 no. 1 appears as a precise compilation of elements from op. 33 no. 5 and op. 54 no. 1: a thematic "motto" which is variously modified, and this in a virtuoso concertant guise, maintaining the unity and strength of the development from a main motive within the fulfillment of that motive's changing character. The concertant elements of the G major *andantino* let the 'non-connoisseurs' forget that Haydn here (a rare case) also works out the slow movement in sonata form. The forceful character of the minuet is spiced with harmonic modulation and metric displacements as well as hemiolic structures. The F major quartet op. 74 no. 2 has a first movement of quite large proportions, characterized by an introductory unison passage, fermatas, contrapuntal theme concentration and harmonic shifts, a very chromatic variation movement with concertant sections, a minuet with a trio in the remote and romantically tinged key of D♭ major, and a *presto* finale, in which symphonic elements mix with polyphonic detail work. Finally, the g minor quartet op.

39 Ibid., *loc. cit.*, 281.

74 no. 3 reaches back to monothematic techniques that Haydn tested in the op. 50 quartets and that remained at his disposal (to which the experimental style did not contribute). This was an optimal compositional technique tried in every way, preserved for every situation, but more as a contrast to the repertoire of technical variants, always expanding the structural and formal possibilities without bringing form so radically into question as in op. 20.

Haydn's last quartets, op. 76, 77 and 103, were written after the second London visit, in the years 1797, 1799 and 1802. The B$^\flat$ major *andante* and d minor minuet of the two movement fragment op. 103 probably were to have served as the middle of a d minor quartet that Haydn was no longer able to complete. Apart from this, these eight quartets (op. 76: no. 1 in G major, no. 2 in d minor, no. 3 in C major, no. 4 in B$^\flat$ major, no. 5 in D major, no. 6 in E$^\flat$ major; op. 77: no. 1 in G major, no. 2 in F major) form a compendium of Haydnesque quartet art — Reginald Barrett-Ayres quite rightly entitled the corresponding chapters of his book "The Harvest" and "Consummation."[40] At this point — and again later — there is apparent a basic problem in our presentation: genre history and evolution here must defer to the compositional importance and the analytical demands of the individual work. This situation deserves a broad exposition, for which this, however, is not the place — these brief remarks on the individual works can only function here to stimulate the reader to make his own more intensive investigation of these quartets, and to give him but a few of the essential points.

The op. 76 quartet cycle, written in 1797 and dedicated to Count Erdödy, continues the tendency begun in op. 71 and 74 toward delineation of individual formal characters,

40 *Ibid.*, 297–312; 340–355.

and it shows, as Ludwig Finscher writes, "noteworthy esthetic undertones, in the deceptive 'genre music' sound of the sonata movement themes, in the scherzo-like *presto* minuets, and above all in the partly coloristic, partly seeming naive thematic material and its elaboration with daring shifts and harmonic subtleties."[41] Thus the first movement of the G major quartet op. 76 no. 1 begins soloistically (after a two measure 'curtain raiser') and is 'filled out' little by little with contrapuntal elements dominating the development. The coda, despite all its songfullness, forms a second development section: the *adagio sostenuto* of this quartet combines *cantabile* and concertant principles and, in the subtle harmonic alterations of the accompaniment under an unchanging theme, bears witness to the above described esthetic. The *presto* minuet has a scherzo character that points clearly to Beethoven. The trio is a contrasting concertant and treble dominated *Ländler*. The finale begins in a serious, thematically tight g minor, its virtuosity growing out of a single thematic germ-cell, with figurative-motivic fragmentation and, here and there, flights of figurative work in flashing facets of sound. Harmonic shifts belie the finale character, first attained rather late in the movement with a brightening turn to major, and a definite turn in the direction of virtuoso demands. The d minor quartet op. 76 no. 2 is similarly constructed, and is related in tone to the g minor quartet op. 20 no. 3. The first movement is composed thematically of the omnipresent interval of the fifth, which in its twofold sequence takes on a thematic character and, in the development, is inverted like a fugue theme, set in stretto with itself and combined with its complementary interval, the fourth. But Haydn does not forget contrasts: after this intellec-

41 Ludwig Finscher "Streichquartett," *MGG*, vol. 12, col. 1568.

tually condensed *allegro* he follows with the D major *andante*, an almost simple rondo movement, a deceptive idyll between the *allegro* and the following "demonic" minuet. This movement, often called the "*Hexenmenuett*," is an endless two voice canon at the octave, while the contrasting D major trio is harmonically refined, and built on a falling scale. The last movement is based melodically on a Slovak folk tune, wedding charming harmonic friction to the rigidity of the original tune. As opposed to the expressive intensity of the first two quartets, the C major quartet op. 76 no. 3, known for its chorale style variations, has a somewhat superficial, glittery, and more symphonic effect, even if the first movement presents a masterpiece of technique in the multiplicity of motivic characters. The B♭ major quartet on the other hand, which anticipates the melody and harmony of advanced chromaticism (in particular Wagner's "Tannhäuser" motive), is definitely among those works where variety of expression and structural differentiation are a perfect unity. This can already be seen in the first measures of the *allegro* with the melodic flight of the first violin over the harmonic background of the other three instruments.

Example 9

The final three movements determine the poetic-expressive tone of this work. The E♭ major *adagio* is a chromatic hymn full of "romantic" harmonies. The minuet, which anticipates Schubertian tonal ordering, is paired with an almost organal trio. The B♭ major finale combines last-dance climax and refined sonata rondo technique. In the D major quartet op. 76 no. 5, Haydn reaches back to the "lighter" character of other last works within this cycle, and in op. 9, 17 and 33. He begins, as also in op. 76 no. 6, with a variation movement, here a 6/8 *Siciliano,* corresponding to the finale of Mozart's d minor quartet KV 421. The F♯ major *largo* is touched with the brightly iridescent character of this rarely used key (and intensified by the major-minor shift). Rounding out the work are a minuet (thematically related to the slow movement) which is rhythmically intricate with many hemiolic constructions, a trio without upper voice, and a *buffo* finale. The E♭ major quartet op. 76 no. 6 continues in this vein. It also opens with a variation movement, which is 'encumbered' by a double fugato, and has as well a B major *fantasia.* This movement, quite startling in its harmonic changes — revolving mainly about semitone relationships (B major/B♭ major/b♭ minor/A♭ major/B major) — is the central point of the quartet. The *presto* minuet is striking on account of unusual melodic leaps in the first violin. In place of the minuet there appears an *alternativo,* where Haydn in a very small space issues a compendium of his superior fugal art, rich in free fantasy, in the contrapuntal setting of a simple falling scale, and out of which he develops the theme of the last movement.

Haydn's last two quartets, joined as op. 77, were written in 1799 and are dedicated to Prince Lobkowicz, who later entered music history as Beethoven's patron and dedicatee of his op. 18 and 74 quartets. The G major quartet op. 77 no. 1 is monothematic with a brief lyric episode developed out of the dotted main motif of the theme; the harmonic modulations and the close connection of dotted rhythms and triplets again anticipate Schubert or, better, they show

how much Schubert's quartet style, so different from that of Beethoven, goes back to Haydn. Thus the function of Haydn's quartets as model for both Beethoven and Schubert secures their exemplary place. The three part E^b major *adagio* combines successive and developmental principles, distinguishes clearly between treble dominated and tutti texture, and likewise anticipates Schubert in its harmonic shifts. The minuet is a quick virtuoso character piece; but the trio, in the mediant tonality of E^b major, plays the role of the rough-hewn, folksy element, while the finale displays anew that compositional principle invented by Haydn — the sonata rondo. In the F major quartet op. 77 no. 2, the central point of the entire cycle is found in the songful D major *andante* which, with its unbounded peacefulness and harmonious balance belongs among the most beautiful of Haydn's variation movements. The important main theme of the first movement is worked out by means of various reduction and fragmentation techniques, and dominates the development almost exclusively. A prolonged epilog section in the recapitulation shows developmental elements and illustrates once again Haydn's high technical and structural standards. Figurative work with sonata elements determines the texture of the minuet, contrasting with a romantic, very legato, B^b major trio. These are the more Romantic elements in the quartet. In particular the technique of expressly contrasting ranges, supported by the renewed median key connection and the variation in style and textural density, are structural principles that win out over more intellectual thematic work and the sonorous element of the homogeneous string texture. These principles won acceptance and achieved importance in the nineteenth century, especially in the national schools, and also played a large role in the twentieth century, with Bartók, Janáček and Berg. It is noteworthy that Haydn here still plays with the sequence of movements placing the minuet second.

Haydn's string quartets — presented here in a cursory overview primarily emphasizing the evolution of the genre — not only form the classical compendium of string quartet art, with a multiplicity of masterpieces, colorfully, structurally and sonorously captivating; they are also the point of departure for the various developments of the genre in the nineteenth and twentieth centuries. In these three ways Haydn's quartets can be prized as models of the genre, and their creator as father of the string quartet.

Luigi Boccherini

As recent research has rightly shown,[1] Luigi Boccherini ranks equally and independently with Joseph Haydn as creator of the string quartet genre. Boccherini, born 1743 in Lucca, published his first works in 1761 at the Parisian house of Vénier.[2] These pieces, probably written while Boccherini was in Lucca, already show complete technical mastery. No continous development such as is found in Haydn's quartets can be traced. It seems that this type of string quartet was born fully grown, with outside influences scarcely perceptible. "Remnants of the forms and inflections of the trio sonata are indeed to be found, but the transparent, refined four voice texture of the chamber music idiom — which Haydn first arrived at only much later — is fully developed, along with the characteristic inflections and sure handling of form. (Boccherini's intimate soloistic familiarity with the cello contributed to its emancipation from the basso continuo.) From the very first, Boccherini writes in a cantabile-concertant style,

1 Yves Gerard, *Thematic, bibliographical and critical catalogue of the works of Luigi Boccherini* (London, 1969); Germaine de Rothschild, *Luigi Boccherini: his life and works* (London, 1965); Alfredo Bonaccorsi, "Luigi Boccherini e il quartetto," in A. Damerini and G. Roncaglia, eds., *Musiche italiane rare e vive* (Siena, 1962).

2 Published under the title *Six Quatuors, opus I, dédiés aux veritables Dilettantes et Connaisseurs en musique,* ed. Vénier (Paris, 1767).

with all four instruments virtually equal in rank. He used a multiplicity of combinations, freely making virtuoso demands and combining the most varied techniques, from strict counterpoint to melodic homophony. Grace and elegance, often with an undertone of gentle melancholy, dominate the melodic writing, along with a second essential element, a very finely nuanced harmony, working subtly with major and minor shadings."[3] This typical style, expressed perhaps most perfectly in Boccherini's first quartet in c minor op. 2 no. 1, and found in the following ones as well, remains almost unchanged and uninfluenced through all the 91 quartets that he composed between 1761 and 1804.[4] This stylistic unity indeed depended mostly on the geographic isolation of the composer: since 1769 he was *kapellmeister* to the Spanish Infante Don Luis, after whose death in 1785 he became *kapellmeister* to the Marquis Bonavente as well as court composer to the Prussian king Friedrich Wilhelm in Madrid. Unlike Haydn, whose work in Esterhazy and Eisenstadt did not isolate him from the musical mainstream, Boccherini's chamber works do not show the influence of musical developments in Germany, France and Italy. Boccherini's tenacious hold on a unified style of writing, touched melodically by the 'galant' sound, may have contributed to the fact that this composer, renowned during his liftetime, fell into oblivion shortly after his death, and soon receded into the niche of a well polished genre and salon music master. This was perhaps encouraged by reduction of the repertory to a vulgarized minuet,

3 Ludwig Finscher, Pamphlet accompanying the recorded selections from Boccherini's op. 32 (Telefunken, 6.35337), 2.

4 See Gerard, *op. cit.*

and the B♭ major cello concerto, disfigured by Friedrich Grützmacher. Only in the last few years has musicology rediscovered Boccherini as a contemporary and, in a certain sense, a rival of Haydn, and only recently has his historical and esthetic significance for the string quartet been rightly appreciated.

Boccherini's 91 quartets, which were published between 1768 and 1806 in Paris by Vénier, La Chevardière, Sieber and Pleyel, present a colorful picture with respect to form. The classical four movement plan did not hold sway: indeed the op. 2 quartets are all in three movements in the sequence fast-slow-fast. The cycles of op. 15 (1772), op. 22 (1775), op. 33 (1781), op. 48 (1794) and op. 53 (1796), designated as "Quartettini" in the manuscript index, are all in two movements, most having a minuet in second place. Quartets in five movements (as in op. 32 no. 2 of 1780) are also found. In variety of movement types the quartets of Boccherini are a constrast to the unified evolution found in Haydn. "The traditional Italian and French forms (of the latter especially the *rondeau*) were taken as finished frames, within which the free fantasy work finds its own boundaries. These forms are taken over, tried in ever new combinations, often broken up by insertions, repetitions and contrasts, but never fundamentally questioned, and never, as in the Viennese classic style, given new meaning through thematic elaboration."[5] The tendency toward multiple variations on technical convention is set in opposition to strictness of compositional layout such as became almost absolute in the theory and esthetics of the nineteenth century especially. And it may have been owing to the normative force of this

5 Finscher, *loc. cit.*, 3.

point of view toward elimination of all deviations that Boccherini's music went unappreciated for so long.

The negligible stylistic evolution within Boccherini's quartet production makes a detailed analysis possible only by contrasting of his own quartets. Variously altered forms, techniques and sounds, as well as different stylistic levels are found analogously in all the quartets. Originality results less from the logical succession of individual evolutionary steps than from the juxtaposition of individual formal developments of a similar kind. Boccherini's first string quartet in c minor op. 2 no. 1 in three movements, will serve here as an example of the early works. An *allegro comodo* and an *allegro* frame an E$^\flat$ major *adagio*. The beginning of the first movement already shows Boccherini's perfect ability to write a cantabile movement while changing and varying the melodic leading in all the voices — a technique of "open work" found only much later in Haydn.

Example 10A

The structure of the first movement is quite characteristic. Instead of a sonata form movement, Boccherini
writes an expanded binary form (m. 1–33, m. 34–74),
with quasi-development motivic variations as well as
insertions of new material, set apart through discontinui-
ty from their metrically and harmonically regular environ-
ment. Each of the two parts exhibits several theme or
motive groups, which for the most part are contrasted
by changing instrumentation. Paired voice leading is
particularly favored — as in m. 17–20, where a section
with second violin and viola is framed by a section with
first violin and cello in its upper register, and also in the
coda-like groups of themes at m. 24–33, where the viola
alone is excluded from the virtuoso figuration. What sets
off the expanded middle section from the beginning is
not so much the development (derived from expository
thematic material), but more harmonic, technical and —
in m. 52–56 — expressive contrapuntal variations that

also contrast dynamically with the particularly cantabile tone of the movement.

The second movement is in four sections in the sequence A-B-C-B. After an opening section with aria-like embellishments, with a first violin melody later recalled unaltered by the cello in its upper register (m. 1–16), there follows a tersely constructed second section, which in its succession of two measure groups and increasing melodiousness creates a clear contrast (also emphasized through the use of the dominant key B$^\flat$ major). The third section (m. 37–55) has, in contrast to the surrounding sections, a strong developmental character, and rather than presenting finished motives, instead lets them arise in varied succession from a continous harmonic texture (m. 37–40) or out of contrary intervallic motion (m. 44ff.). The fourth section (m. 56–76), on the other hand, is identical with the second until the alteration of the harmonic descent to the tonic.

With 181 *alla breve* measures, the third movement is almost twice as long as the first two. Also unlike the first movement, whose minor character was tempered by major thirds and raised sevenths, Boccherini works here with the rugged expressive minor (comparable with the middle symphonies of Haydn) that this key was associated with in the second half of the eighteenth century. This movement exhibits no regular sonata form, but throughout makes use of developmental sections. It is divided overall into two large, seven part blocks (m. 1–80, m. 114–181), between which those developmental sections are found. The principle of contrast governs the entire movement: after a stolid unison beginning with dotted rhythms and melodic descent (m. 1–10), there follows a *dolce expressivo* cantabile section for the first violin accompanied by the other instruments (m. 11—18). The third section uses both these elements and adds the contrapuntal crossing of the upper three parts and obligato chaconne character as a third structural element (m. 19—27). The adjacent fugue with a clearly homophonic interlude is framed by a section of canon between the first violin and cello (m. 50—55) and a graceful coda, in which the composer again indulges his liking for paired voice leading (m. 56—71). The developmental middle section (m. 81—114), where the 'chaconne section' is recalled (m. 87—92 corresponding to m. 19ff.), alters motivic elements of the fugue theme in an expansive homophonic texture, now without having the character of an intermezzo; from m. 114 on, the first section is repeated with the 'chaconne section,' unaltered save for some harmonic rearrangement.

The op. 58 no. 2 quartet in E♭ major will serve as a second example, for within this cycle, the last one printed (1799) in the composer's lifetime, there is a fundamental departure from the style prevailing earlier. Ludwig Finscher characterized it thus: "they experiment with irregular three movement layout and, in the first violin, show influences of the French violin school, along with emotional intensity in the orchestral volume, and a tendency towards extreme juxtaposition (semitone shifts and violent dynamic contrasts) — all these being the somewhat refined effects on quartet style of the music of the French revolution."[6] The quartet in E♭ major, in four movements, with a surprising indication of *allegro lento* for the first movement, is a mixture of variation technique, elements of sonata-like development and something of a vocal 'scene.' Songlike themes, and regular phrase formation

6 Finscher, "Streichquartett," *MGG*, vol. 12, col. 1574.

alternate with recitative-like interludes, counterposing the 'discursive' melody of the first violin with a uniform accompaniment. Extreme dynamic contrast and brilliant virtuoso effects in all four instruments (but favoring the first violin and cello) result in an almost orchestral sound. The minuet, in second place, has a scherzo character expressed in irregular phrase structure, stress on offbeats and contrapuntal condensation. The trio is scarcely a contrasting movement: it renounces the usual genre characteristics and strives more for a many-layered acoustic perspective, analogous to the trio of Mozart's $B^\flat$ major quartet KV 589. The *larghetto* third movement is in a lingering, melancholy melodic style at its most conventional, though it broadens its expressive range with highly pathetic unison effects. The finale is on a similar level of complexity: a loose sonata rondo construction is here amalgamated with fugal elements. Thus the two part fugal beginning, reminiscent of the beginning of the song *"Ah! vous dirais-je maman"* combines a broad motto type beginning with figured thematic answers. The contrapuntal character of this movement is nevertheless not maintained throughout but rather gives way to virtuoso treble-dominated texture or, in harmonic progression, to orchestral tonal effects.

Example 10B

One should be able to see from this analysis wherein Boccherini's specific compositional ability lay, namely in the use and combination of a great variety of heterogeneous formal types and compositional elements, in

69

obvious contrasts and subtly shaded transformations. Thematic elaboration is seldom found; rather there is more a kaleidoscopic interchange of various textural levels and a charming, almost montage-like concatenation of independent structural units. Many have been accustomed to fix the evolution of the string quartet solely in the lineage of Haydn-Beethoven-Brahms-Schoenberg, as early as Louis Spohr, who pronounced adverse criticism on the character of Boccherini's works, or Robert Eitner, who judged: "unfortunately he wrote hastily, examined little and wrote, among rather good works, many worthless ones."[7] With such a viewpoint, Boccherini could hardly be properly understood as Haydn's opposite number. But recent research, as Ludwig Finscher writes, has come to an historically correct answer: "Convention is the secure foundation on which musical fantasy can play freely, as long as it never oversteps the bounds of good taste: above all in deliberate, indeed endless testing of detail, in light melancholy submersion into the particular feeling of a work, with strictest observation of etiquette and 'bon gout,' Boccherini attained a musical stature unique to himself, at the same time appearing as the perfect representative of the last prerevolutionary epoch."[8] The source and documentary situation is quite good for the researcher on account of the preliminary work of Yves Gerard,[9] but less

7 Quoted from "Boccherini," *MGG*, vol. 2, col. 5.

8 Finscher, *loc. cit.*, 3.

9 See note 1.

so for the musician. Of Boccherini's 91 string quartets only a good third exist in new printings, and these editions
are in part unreliable, especially in matters of dynamics
and articulation. But a complete edition being prepared in
Italy[10] should, if slowly, improve the situation.

10 *Le opere complete di L. Boccherini*, ed. Instituto italiano per la storia della
musica (Rome, 1970); the quintets and quartets have been edited for the
most part by Pina Carmirelli, first violinist of the Boccherini Quartet in
Italy, with the aim of a more widespread and intensive cultivation of
Boccherini's music.

Wolfgang Amadeus Mozart

Mozart's 23 authentic string quartets were written between 1770 and 1790,[1] and thus should be considered
with reference to the earlier or contemporary quartets
of Haydn (up to op. 55). The first quartet in the form for
the most part stabilized by that time was the work of the
fourteen year old Mozart during March of 1770 in Lodi
in northern Italy. The three movement G major quartet
KV 80, in the sequence *adagio-allegro-menuetto,* shows
the influence of the instrumental music of Giuseppe
Sammartini: the paired voice leading of both violins, the
close coupling of the viola with the bass, the bass function
of the cello (retained up to the mature quartets). All these
elements document a standard for the genre that lags
somewhat behind the chronologically earlier quartets of
Boccherini or Haydn. A *Rondeau*[2] was composed later to
expand the work to four movements.

1 The editions within the *Neuen Mozart-Ausgabe* should be consulted for
   analyses (Kassel 1958ff.); series 8, *Werkgruppe* 20, vols. 1–3; vol. 1 (KV
   80–173) edited by Karlheinz Füssl, Wolfgang Rehm and Wolfgang Plath
   (Kassel 1966); vol. 2 (KV 387–464) and 3 (KV 465–590) edited by
   Ludwig Finscher (Kassel 1964); of which see the pocket score edition in
   one volume, Kassel 1964 *Taschenpartitur* no. 140.

2 On this subject see the foreword to the *NMA* (cited above), ix; Abert,
   Mozart (Leipzig, 1966), vol. 1,348; Alfred Einstein, *Mozart – sein Charakter und Werk* (Stockholm, 1947), 239. In an article that appeared after
   the completion of this manuscript, "Mozarts erstes Streichquartett: Lodi,
   15. März 1770," *Analecta musicologia* vol. 18, *Mozart und Italien* (Cologne, 1978), 246–270, Ludwig Finscher sought another meaning of the
   quartet and understood it as a kind of *"réunion des gouts"*, in which the
   young Mozart – feeling quite at home in all areas – combined with each
   other Italian trio sonata (first movement), Italian sinfonia (second movement), Austrian dance-minuet (third movement) and French rondeau
   (fourth movement).

Mozart's first quartet cycle originated in the winter of 1772–73 during a rather long stay in Salzburg. These works are also in three movements throughout (fast-slow-fast), with minuet-like dance movements acting as finales in KV 156 and 158. The clear tonal plan of the cycle (D major, G major, C major, F major, B$^\flat$ major E$^\flat$ major) in a falling circle of fifths indicates the quasi-programmatic character of this group. Unlike the rather orchestrally conceived[3] KV 80 and the KV 136–138 divertimentos written in the summer of 1772, we have here Mozart's first formally dedicated quartets. Structural experimentation – as in Haydn's quartets of op. 9, 17 and 20 – are not found in the work of the young Mozart. The sonata movements are thoroughly regular and subscribe to the formal canon of the time. Development sections are brief, constructed for the most part of short imitative passages, with episodic, subordinate second themes largely overshadowed by virtuoso codas. A pronounced contrast between the individual themes, as in the second cycle KV 168–173, is not yet found here, but in its place among the motivic groups are internal contrasts of dynamics, melody and harmony. The slow movements – mostly in the dominant (KV 155, 160) or parallel minor (KV 156–159) – are ornamented instrumental arias in a three part canzona style. Their middle sections show some developmental moments and differ chiefly in harmony from the surrounding parts. Still frequently perceptible are elements of the Baroque trio sonata, as in KV 157. In neither dynamics nor texture is there yet discernable a manner of writing expressly specific to the string quartet genre.

3 See on this subject the foreword to the *NMA*, vii and passim; also the editor's foreword "Zu den Quartett-Divertimenti KV 136–138" in *NMA* series iv, *Werkgruppe* 12, vol. 6 (Kassel, 1970), viiff., and Ludwig Finscher "Streichquartett" *MGG*, vol. 12, col. 1570.

Orchestral or loose, divertimento-like techniques are combined with genuine chamber music writing. The first movement of the C major quartet KV 157 for example, with its *piano* and *forte* recall of the main theme, takes up tried and true orchestral effects of the "Mannheim" style throughout, as well as the beloved crescendo-*walze* and the festive *'coup d'archet'* that Mozart would still use effectively in his symphony KV 297. In addition, the final rondos (KV 155, 157, 159) are modeled on the earlier south German and Austrian divertimento. Expressions of a specific, individual style occur most frequently in the area of harmony: for example, in the key relationship of F major-a minor-F major/minor in KV 158, or in the slow movement of the E$^\flat$ major quartet KV 160 which obscures the initial tonality by opening on the seventh.

Example 11

The second work of the cycle, the G major quartet KV 156, may be examined somewhat more closely here as a representative example: the 3/8 presto is rather divertimento-like (as the movement's marking already indicates[4]) in its sequence of two and four measure groupings, its emphasis on the upper voice and its use of unison effects. The development is short and restricted to imitative combinations and repetitions without any thematic work. Since the recapitulation repeats the exposition material unaltered, one can regard this type of movement as something between the 'ABA' type based on contrast, and the development sonata-allegro movement. The e minor *adagio* is of the arioso-figurative type, and likewise rather more orchestral than chamber musical in its use of voice exchange and unisons. Expressive, operatic chromaticism dominates the middle section (m. 15—19) of this tripartite movement. The finale, an expanded dance movement in G major/g minor is based on internal thematic contrasts, and the beginnings of a solid, imitative texture.

4 See above p. 26 regarding the development of movement tempos in Haydn.

It is noteworthy that Mozart took over the head motive as well as the accompaniment figure of the trio for the opening material of his minuet in the late B^b major quartet KV 589.

The works which became known as the "Milan" quartets, and which for a long time were attributed to Mozart under the Köchel numbers *anhang 210—213,* have been identified by Ludwig Finscher as the works of Joseph Schuster.[5]

The second of Mozart's quartet cycles, again comprising the traditional number of six works, was written just a year later, during Mozart's stay in Vienna in the autumn of 1773. In the interim he had become acquainted with Haydn's quartets op. 17 and op. 20 published in 1771 and 1772, and Mozart's six new quartets (F major KV 168, A major KV 169, C major KV 170, E major KV 171, B^b major KV 172 and d minor KV 173) reflect the seventeen year old's coming to grips with Haydn's models, as is shown clearly in very frequent imitations and borrowings (though not yet in individualized transformation and reshaping). Having outgrown the role of child prodigy, Mozart was at that time experiencing a creative crisis. His acquaintance with the works of Haydn (much as his acquaintance with the works of Bach ten years later) shook him free of a somewhat naive compositional attitude, stimulating from without the growth of a new style.

The overall plan of the six new quartets is clearly large-scale: not only did Mozart here use four movement plans exclusively for the first time (the last movement of KV 80 was probably composed contemporaneously with these quartets, in order to bring that early work

5   Ludwig Finscher, "Mozarts *'Mailänder'* Streichquartette," *MF* 19 (1966).

'up to date'), but he also enlarged the individual movements, increased the 'weight' of the first movement (as expressed in slower tempos) and finally he rethought the character of the slow movements, giving them more particular importance, and made the dance movements more concise. All this accomplished an evolutionary step, which had been taken by Haydn several years earlier in the progression from op. 1 and 2 to op. 9 and 17. A final problem remained, however. Unlike Haydn, Mozart's use of contrapuntal techniques (as in the final fugues of KV 168 and 173) is not an experimental attempt to solve a formal problem, but rather the imitation of the model of Haydn's op. 20. Accordingly, Mozart's fugues do not have that character of breaking through structural boundaries, and instead remain in that Baroque style of one trained in the church music and fugue-quartets of a Monn or a Tume — a style that stays strongly impersonal and scholastic, enlivened with only a little homophonic interplay. The chromatic fugue in KV 173 is not a herald of Mozart's late and excessive fugal harmony (such as in KV 546) but rather restricts itself to the use of chromatic elements in a diatonic setting. Here, the otherwise quite advanced harmonic practice is actually thoroughly conventional.

Unconventional in many ways, however, is the structure of the slow movements, particularly in the inclusion of muted sounds (in KV 168 and 171), the use of canon, and the choice of expressive minor coloring. These three elements, although certainly inspired by Haydn (cf. the *andante* in op. 20 no. 5), also illustrate the composer's own individual tendencies. The slow movements of the quartets KV 169 and 171, both generally less tightly structured, are on the other hand either serenade-like (KV 171) or an arioso-opera type with upper voice dominating. Rather different is the organization of the movements in the C major quartet KV 170. Mozart here reaches back to the prototype of Haydn's op. 17 no. 3 and begins the work with a series of slow variations, in which a clearly structured cantabile theme is figuratively unfolded, without its being further developed and without a variation in minor. The actual slow movement, partitioned off by the second movement minuet, remains in a canzona-like serenade style. Also departing from the scheme is the sequence of movements in the d minor quartet KV 173. Here an *andantino grazioso* in rondo form takes the place of the slow movement — a type of movement more likely to have functioned as a finale. The inconsistency of the solutions to the problem of the last movement has already been pointed out. Along with the two fugues are found two multi-sectional rondos (KV 169 and 170), as well as two movements with the character and tempo of a loosely constructed sonata allegro (KV 171 and 172). This is a further witness to the stylistic distinction between the two cycles — the last movement of KV 171 is comparable throughout in rhythm, tempo and form with the first movement of KV 156 analyzed above.

The thirteen early string quartets of Mozart show those distinctly different starting points for development of the genre that characterize the production of the younger composer, and set it apart from that of the older Haydn. Mozart carried out a step by step emancipation of a string quartet style from orchestral and divertimento elements not in a uniquely technical way, but rather in his own adaptation of the current, 'state of the art' chamber musical situation. If in 1770 this was still for him the northern Italian instrumental style of Sammartini, then three years later it was the influence of Joseph Haydn.

79

Up to the present the six quartets dedicated to Joseph Haydn have determined Mozart's rank as a quartet composer. They came about, as Mozart wrote in the dedication to Haydn, as the fruit "of a long and difficult labor" between the beginning of 1782 and the turn of 1784–85, and were published in September 1785 by Artaria in Vienna as op. 10 (not assigned by Mozart). What the op. 20 quartets were to the cycle KV 168–173, so Haydn's op. 33 quartets, which appeared in 1782, were the stimulating impulse for this new group. Not only their collective publication after so long a period of gestation, but numerous compositional details also show that they were planned from the start as a self-contained and integral cycle. Yet compared with the model/emulator situation of a good ten years earlier, the relationship is now quite different. "The acquaintance with these quartets of Haydn made one of the deepest impressions upon Mozart's artistic life. But this time he did not let himself be overwhelmed. This time he learned as master from master. He didn't copy; he gave up nothing of his own individuality."[6]

The dedication of the six quartets to Haydn was not simply an extreme expression of gratitude; it set up at the same time an intentional comparison with the great model. This is confirmed by Haydn's famed statement to Leopold Mozart in spring 1785 after he heard the quartets in a private performance arranged for him. Leopold Mozart reported the remark in a letter to his daughter in Salzburg. Haydn said: "I say to you before God, as an honorable man, that your son is the greatest composer that I know personally or by reputation. He has taste and, what is more, the greatest skill in composition." Taste

6 Alfred Einstein, *Mozart. Sein Charakter. Sein Werk.* (Frankfurt, 1968), 251.

and skill in composition — in these quartets the two complementary concepts are brought inimitably down to a single denominator. And whoever still believes the fable of the beloved-of-God Mozart, to whom ideas simply flowed, is advised to study the autograph of these six quartets. They show more clearly than any words how much *"Kompositionswissenschaft"* was a necessary ingredient — even if not perceived by superficial listening.

Contemporary public reaction was reserved, or even negative toward the publication of the quartets (in contrast to the positive reception for Haydn's works). Thus one reads in a periodical critic: "A pity that Mozart in his artful and effectively beautiful composition climbs too high in his effort to become a new creator, whereby he achieves little indeed of heartfelt feeling. His new quartets, which he has dedicated to Haydn, are too strongly spiced — and what palate can long endure that?"[7] The all-too-strong "spice" was probably tasted in the first place in the slow introduction of the C major quartet KV 465, which occasioned all sorts of other displeasure as well,[8] on account of its harsh dissonances, thoroughly explicable nevertheless as sequential suspensions and passing tones, and therefore not endangering the tonal stability.

In contrast to Haydn's experimental (in the modern sense) compositional technique, there are in Mozart's six quartets (G major KV 387, written in December 1782; d minor KV 421, June 1783, E♭ major KV 428, summer 1783; B♭ major KV 458, December 1784; C

7 *Cramers Magazin der Musik*, II, 1273ff.

8 See: Antoine-Elysee Cherbuliez, "Zur harmonischen Analyse der Einleitung von Mozarts C-Dur-Quartett" in *Bericht über die musikal. Tagung der Int. Stiftung Mozarteum August 1931* (Leipzig, 1932), 103—111. Otto Erich Deutsch, "Sartis Streitschrift gegen Mozart," *Mozart-Jahrbuch* (1962/63), 7—13.

major KV 465, January 1785) scarcely any large scale formal or structural peculiarities that would distinguish his works from their Haydn model. It is much more thematic details, particularly the harmonic variety within the smallest space, the frequent shifts between major and minor and the somewhat melancholy-major quality quite unique to Mozart that establish the charm and value of these quartets.

These quartets are in four movements throughout. The placement of the minuet varies, not out of fundamental formal deliberation, but depending on the function of the dance movement as a bridge or equalizing element between the different, weighty expressions of the first movement and the slow movement. So (as in KV 387 or 464) the minuet stands in second place when the main compositional weight lies in the slow movement, or when (as in KV 421) a tempo equalization is to be created. It stands in third place where the slow movements — mostly marked *andante* — are rather *cantabile* and *concertant* in tempo and character.

If the individuality of these compositions does not result mainly from formal experimentation, realizations of it can nevertheless be seen which are not yet to be found in Haydn (but which do however point out clearly Haydn's influence). In the G major quartet KV 387, there are two main experimental elements: one is Mozart's use of sonata form for all four movements, the other is the new approach to the use of fugue and sonata-allegro principles in the finale.[9] Important above all is the tight cyclic linking of the four movements through melodic emphasis on the scalar interval of the fourth and its

9 See Reginald Barrett-Ayres, *Joseph Haydn and the string quartet* (London, 1974), 190f.

continual chromatic "filling in," best illustrated perhaps in the consequent phrase of the minuet theme. This melodic chromaticism in particular, many examples of which are found throughout all six quartets, embraces the whole cycle, helping to form a compositional "arch."

What differentiates Mozart's technique of development and elaboration from Haydn's can likewise be seen readily in an example from the first movement of KV 387. While with Haydn thematic development is mostly a matter of dissolution, of the reduction of larger units into small motives combined with each other in a variety of ways, with Mozart this development almost always springs from harmonic sources, as the horizontalization of a vertical chord, its dissolution found in a melodic expression. Thus with Mozart the distinction between dissolution of motivic work and figuration can often be far from clear. One need only compare the beginning of the exposition and that of the development of the first movement of KV 387:

Example 12

M. 56

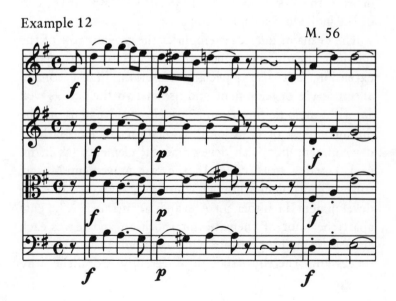

A very playfully applied adaptation of Haydn's technique is the use of small insertions (in part thematically derived, in part extra-thematic) within the course of the movement, so-called *"devisen"* or mottos such as Haydn used, for example, at the very beginning of op. 33 no. 5 or as in the first movement of Mozart's KV 387 at the end of the individual sonata sections.

The G major quartet exemplifies the growing role of the minuet, already mentioned with regard to its temporal extension, but also especially important in the sonata-allegro style development and use of two themes, as well as with melodic inversion. The slow movement in the dominant key of C major is a sonata movement without development but with developmental elements (as in m. 6–12) and a brief coda. In the last movement Mozart solves the problem of joining contrapuntal and sonata-type development in rather an Alexandrian manner — he cuts apart the knot of thematic interposition and leaves each element in its proper state while combining them in quick succession, thereby (though differently from the way

Haydn would have done it) aiming at the lighter *'capriccio'* character of the finale. The main theme of the sonata movement is in two parts, as are almost all themes within these Haydn quartets. The first part, four whole notes at intervals of a third, fourth and third, is fugally conceived; the second is an almost primitive chain of eighths in the first violin, constructed of simple, homophonic cadence formulas. Nevertheless these allow for a contrapuntal interconnection of individual subsections. A second fugal section is presented and combined several times with the first in the form of a double fugue. The episodic secondary theme on the contrary, which entered relatively late (m. 91ff.), is purely homophonic, as is the codetta to the exposition, with a chromatic transitional figure harking back to the minuet. Since the extended fugue section in the exposition already had a development character, the actual development (m 125 to 174) has been kept relatively brief.

While in the G major quartet KV 387 it was in the first place constructive characteristics that created the work's individuality, the overall effect of the d minor quartet KV 421 is based on expressive qualities that are to be found not only in the specifically Mozartean minor, but also in certain tonal and timbral qualities. Thus the dark, low instrumental range plays a dominant role in the first movement, and the contrasting upper reaches of the first violin are almost always attained only through wide interval leaps. Next to this there is a palpable concentration of structural materials, a very tight, goal-oriented technique, which does altogether without the episodic. The gathering up of compositional perception of time is also expressed in that the true contrast to the gloomily oppressive character of the movement's opening is not found in the second theme, but rather in the peaceful, simple second movement. This F major *andante* has an f minor middle part set off by figuration, but the outer sections, in contrast to the first movement (characterized by thematic work with many rests and small motives, as well as through the use of relatively simple cadences) create, in spite of quantifiable extent, a quite different experience of time. The minuet is a very compact contrapuntal piece with head motive imitation, whose repetition figure in the third measure of the theme appears again in the finale. In the middle section especially it partakes of the chromatic harmony that is a fundamental constituent of all six quartets. The trio, an idyllic serenade, is broken a bit only by the Lombard rhythm of the first violin and its large leaps in the middle section. The first definite citation from Haydn's op. 33 is found in the finale, a variation movement in *Siciliano* rhythm.

Example 13

More interesting than the melodic parallels, however, are the differences between Haydn and Mozart that can already be found in the first measure of the theme and in the various harmonizations. With Haydn, a harmony with a folky popular tone is based on simple cadence successions, but with Mozart, the cello (here clearly assuming the function of *basso continuo*) guarantees the clarity of the overall texture; but in the middle voices, in particular in the latent chromaticism of the second violin, this simplicity is easily upset and given new meaning in detail or brought into question during the course of the development. The variations follow the model familiar from Mozart's piano works: figurative filling out of the theme in the first, metrical shifts and thickening of accompaniment in the second, a brief solo for the viola with reminders of the Lombard rhythms of the trio in the third, and an abbreviated major variation with descending cello flourishes. The only departure from the conventional scheme is the coda which, in a quicker tempo, expands in particular upon the repetitive consequent phrase, introducing something like contrapuntal voice-crossing. The coda is remarkable in its almost playful chromatic shifts in the accompaniment in the last four measures. Thus it is evident here that the value of these quartets is not to be found in formal structure itself, but rather in the very individual (in particular harmonic) fulfillment of the conventional formal schemes.

Like the A major quartet KV 464, the quartet in E major KV 428, written a few weeks later in the summer of 1783, has generally come up a little short in the appreciation of these quartets. This is perhaps because Mozart here wandered the farthest from the path pioneered by Haydn. The unison beginning of the first movement and its continuation in a clearly delineated four voice texture certainly points to its model: but its continuation is a creation of Mozartean individuality. The development is chiefly characterized by its rhythm from the transformation of a turn-motive to the virtuoso chain of triplets displaced through various scales, and running through all the instruments. This section expresses its individual nature in a harmonically distinguished retransition in the recapitulation and in several recapitulation extensions (e.g. m. 109, 157—158) that, much as in the recapitulations of the other quartets in this cycle, are harmónically motivated. The slow movement, *andante con moto,* is certainly the most harmonically rich piece of the whole cycle. In fact, this movement has often been mentioned in connection with that "Tristan chromaticism," or the harmony of a Romantic composer like Brahms.[10] Not only is the harmony irregular here — so is the phrase structure. The first theme is constructed of 1 + 3 + 1 measures, and uneven phrases occur frequently as the work progresses. The subtle cyclic connection of the individual movements is furthered in measure 77: here, as a strong closing flourish, Mozart cites the head motive of the first movement's second theme. The minuet has leanings toward sonata form (if indeed less expressly than that of KV 387), but in place of the development there comes a provocatively simple, repeated cadence figure (m. 27–33). The trio appears to be based harmonically on the cello pedal, yet through chromatic shifting of the inner voices even this is held ever in suspense. The last movement, analogous in its structure to that of KV 465, can be characterized as an abbreviated rondo. Mozart here strikes the same 'tone' as in his Haydn quartets — that unencumbered certainty of goal that, in its very few departures from a regular course, strives for a merely temporary disorientation of the hearer, and otherwise shows the composer to be of one mind with him throughout.

The B$^\flat$ major quartet KV 458, written in November of 1784, is probably the lightest within the cycle. It belongs in third place among the six, according to Mozart's own numbering of the autograph, as opposed to the actual chronology of origin. This is, on the one hand, probably to clarify the tonal connection of d minor/B$^\flat$

---

10 See for example Barrett-Ayres, *loc. cit.,* 195.

major/E^b major, and on the other in order to maintain sufficient richness of expressive contrast in the sequence of works. The added name '*Jagd*' quartet hardly jibes with the work's character: only the key of B^b major and the 'hunt'-like opening might be held responsible for the name. Special attention should be called to the paired voice leading within the quartet (here Mozart aligns himself with rather later models) — and indeed it is carried out to such an extent that the framing sections and inner part are correspondingly opposed to each other. The element of the development are based on the surprising connection and opposition of a triad-motive with following cambiata. Here the thematic development is less interesting than the form of the motive itself which has been altered according to the harmonic function.

Example 14

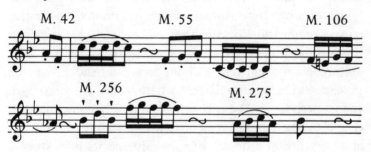

The extended coda to the movement assumes the function of a second development section, as it frequently also does with Haydn. A marginal detail can be pointed out in the first measures of the development (m. 91—97), where the first violin melody contains a motive from the song *"Komm, schöner Mai,"* already used in the B^b major piano concerto KV 595 in an analogous type of movement. Instead of the usual tonal relationship, the minuet and trio are both in B♭ major and are structurally less interesting — except for a chromatic middle voice enrichment (m. 16ff.) that emphasizes the cyclic design. The slow movement, an *adagio*, is a sonata movement without development, clearly featuring the upper voice, but also involving melodic interplay between the first violin and cello and harmonic false relations (m. 14—15; m. 17—18) at the entrance of the second theme, foreshadowing the introduction to the C major quartet. The finale is a brilliantly boistrous sonata allegro, to be understood perhaps as a parody of a 'Haydnesque' movement,[11] with some definitely operatic section endings.

The A major quartet KV 464, composed in close association with the C major quartet KV 465 around the turn of 1784/85, probably found less favor with the public because of the subtlety of compositional means and because, as Alfred Einstein remarked, the "learned" outweighs the *"galante"* a bit. Here Mozart reaches full mastery in contrapuntal permeation of the four voices, and this within a completely developed and thoroughly chromaticized texture almost entirely without the usual successions of cadences. Thus these latter, where they are used, are almost parodistic. The two part, structurally contrary main theme of the first movement (where a simple accompaniment texture of a descending melody and its brief unison answer make up a compact, self-contained motive) forms the thematic germ cell of the whole movement. The secondary theme (only a climbing chromatic line resolving into triplets), remains rather an arabesque. The development brings together a number of different forms in a very small space, all drawing on the same motivic sources but contrasting harmonically, melodically,

11 Barrett-Ayres, *loc. cit.,* 196.

in articulation and dynamics in a scarcely unified way. The minuet, related thematically in the fifth and sixth measures with the minuet from KV 421, once again follows sonata form and cites in its course the closing flourish of the first movement (m. 23/24). The slow movement presents a succession of figurated variations on a simple, songlike theme, ending in the sixth variation and coda over a repeating murky bass that starts in the cello, wanders through the voices, returning finally to the cello and there – to use a modern concept – is, so to speak, phased out. The last movement, though again more subtly than in KV 387, illustrates the Mozartean connection of sonata form and contrapuntal principles. The sonata movement is based on two contrapuntal motives which, as theme and countersubject, are connected with each other from the very beginning, and wherein chromaticism once again plays a role in setting the 'tone.' Unlike the last movement of KV 387 this elegànt final resolution only reveals itself fully upon closer examination; Mozart quite consciously avoids signaling: 'Attention! Here comes a fugue.'

Mozart's last quartet in the cycle dedicated to Haydn has become well known chiefly on account of the dissonances in its *adagio* introduction. These are in the first place expressive dissonances, explainable (as already has been mentioned) as a sequence of suspensions and passing tones within the voice leading and, although it certainly could not have been known to the composer, they form a bridge from the expressive dissonances of the madrigals of Carlo Gesualdo. Besides this, they function as an element of contrast to the almost simple thematic work of the following first movement, and they encompass, from measure 9 in particular, that melodic chromaticism already many times identified as a unifying element of all the quartets. The immediately following sonata movement is thoroughly regular in its layout with an episodic secondary theme dissolving into triplets (m. 71ff.), and a codetta that already shows developmental work. The actual development reaches back to thoroughly contrapuntal techniques — to canonic stretto between the first violin and viola (m. 107—116), the invention of new countersubjects, stating the theme in the bass (m. 122ff.), spinning out and canonic crossing of individual thematic elements between cello and first violin (m. 125—136). The recapitulation is regular but, as in KV 458, adds a codà that, while rather figurative in form, also takes on development function. The slow movement can be identified as a sonata movement without development or as a two part form with decided sonata-type developmental elements in the second part. Here, as already in KV 458, the actual development work makes use of a motive not exposed in the main theme group. In addition, the minuet has the character of a sonata movement throughout, in particular in the opposition of the chromatic motive exposed first (reminiscent of the first movement of KV 464) and the unison motive (also a structural principle from KV 464). To a much less ambitious extent than in KV 464, the finale combines the structural form of a sonata movement with contrapuntal compositional technique, though this is restricted largely to the clearly bounded development. The movement thus has much more of an especially light 'last-dance' character than the A major quartet since Mozart here adheres to diatonicism to an unusual degree.

"These six great quartets by Mozart are not only proof of his inventiveness and virile imagination, but they are also a lasting tribute and memorial to Joseph Haydn, from whom he learned much about the difficult and intricate art of writing for four equal stringed instruments. It is impossible to place one great man before the other. In this case Haydn and Mozart complement each other: one provides a foil for the other, one is serious, the other is jesting, but the next moment the roles are entirely reversed."[12] While the six Haydn quartets of Mozart are a self-contained cycle, an element of isolation can be found in each of the last four quartets. The D major composed in the summer of 1786 in particular is quite an erratic element within a period that saw the creation of the opera *"The Marriage of Figaro"* as well as numerous piano works. The proximity to *"Figaro"* has induced many authors to speak of a relaxed cheerfulness and unproblematic 'filling in' of regular forms. A closer look, however, reveals under the 'untroubled' mask the melancholy and desolation of this composition, which seeks occasionally to give vent to emotion in bizarre formal and structural ways. It seems quite possible that Mozart had here produced an analogue to the likewise isolated and strange d minor quartet op. 42 of Haydn. Mozart nevertheless had characterized his work with formal elements that Haydn subsequently adopted in his op. 50; in particular, the monothematicism of the first movement of KV 499 is found again in Haydn. This tight thematic concentration without episodic secondary themes, and the many varied, transformed main theme motives of the dominant section of the exposition (m. 83ff.) (which moreover enters decidedly late) combine to present a very much lighter textural picture than the Haydn quartets — also resulting from rather frequent use of three or even just two voice texture. This perhaps, next to the melodic simplicity of the theme, has led to the mistaken *"Figaro"* relationship. Quite unusually, the the-

12 Barrett-Ayres, *loc. cit.*, 201.

matic work begins here right after the first measures in the two voice combination of the two theme parts — the descending triad and the dotted upbeat figure. In particular, contrapuntal techniques such as inversion, diminution and stretto provide for an unusually thick textural consistency quite different from its supposed 'transparency.' The real development, only 42 measures long, can concentrate on harmonic work since contrapuntal elaboration is found already in the exposition and later in the recapitulation and coda. This harmonic concentration is carried out to a degree that, in the renunciation of all traditional disposition of keys and unprepared changes (indeed rough shifts) of tonal area, shows a harmonic instability first seen again in the mature works of Schubert — a good forty years later. The minuet as well as the slow movement are related to the Haydn quartets; only the d minor trio with its contrapuntal elaboration and combinative technique asserts its independence. Although the development of the G major *adagio* (a sonata movement) is brief (m. 40—53), it shows numerous developmental areas in its other sections. But these development areas dissolve into figurative garlands in the first violin, and give the movement a concertant character. Finally, the last movement is not only a mixture of sonata movement and rondo that defies analysis, it also shows an expressive changeableness which has led to the most contrary interpretations. Hermann Abert thus identifies the movement as a finale "with sparkling humor"[13] while Alfred Einstein characterizes it quite differently "The finale is again one of those weird movements in which major mode appears to go against its nature — it is not cheerful but, rather, desolate or, better, it is desolate under the mask of cheerfulness despite the resoluteness of the conclusion."[14]

13 Abert, *loc. cit.*, vol. 2, 317.   14 Einstein, *loc. cit.*, 255.

Mozart's three so-called "Prussian" quartets were written in 1789 and 1790 in Vienna and were published shortly after his death, once again by Artaria. (The D major quartet KV 499 was published by Hoffmeister.) Occasion for the composition was a visit in February 1789 to the cellist king of Prussia Wilhelm II in Potsdam. As had Luigi Boccherini (*Hofkapellmeister* since 1787) and also Haydn (in his quartets op. 50) before him, Mozart wished to write six string quartets in order to improve his economic situation with the customary donation in response to his dedication. But it was his economic situation that forced him nevertheless to sell the three finished quartets KV 575, 589 and 590 to Artaria in the summer of 1790 before the completion of the cycle.

The intention to write the quartets for the capable cellist Friedrich Wilhelm II had considerable influence on the plan of the quartets; unlike Haydn, whose op. 50 certainly also favors the cello but does not otherwise deviate from his personal style, the solo function of the cello in these three quartets is clearly a departure from the usual overall structure: here the layout is very much looser and more in a concertant style unrelated to the compositional compactness of the Haydn quartets. The motivic-thematic development proceeds (almost as in a solo concerto) much more slowly, with frequent repetition of formal sections; the decided *cantabile* tone and virtuosity of the themes scarcely allows for intensive motivic or contrapuntal work. Mozart's publisher Artaria was therefore quite correct when he advertised the work in December 1791 as *"Konzertante Quartetten."*

The D major quartet KV 575, written in June 1789, shows the playful, concertant layout of these late works perhaps most clearly: the relatively slow first movement, marked *allegretto,* partakes in both main and secondary theme of a *cantabile* tone and varied theme recalls in all four instruments. The high range of the cello makes it necessary that now and then the second violin or, more frequently, the viola take over the bass function: frequently however, as already seen in KV 499, two and three voice texture emerges without a bass line at all. The development touches on remote keys, if not in such extreme succession as in the D major quartet KV 499, and even presents a new theme (m. 86ff.) — this also an expression of concertant rather than motivic-thematic structure. Apart from isolated instances of voice exchange, the recapitulation proceeds quite regularly. There are in any case scarcely any formal deviations to be found in the first movements of these three quartets, most certainly corresponding to the increasing displacement of compositional 'weight' onto the last movement. The slow movement, with melodic correspondences to Mozart's song *"Das Veilchen,"* is again a sonata movement without development, concentrating on *cantabile*-concertant dialogue, especially between first violin and cello. In adopting the motive of the slow movement's closing flourish, the minuet ties into its expressive character and thus connects the two middle movements into one unit (a situation also found in KV 589 and 590) and clearly separates them from the first movement and the finale. Above all, cyclic unity is clearly shown in the relationship of the head motives of all four movements, as well as in the citation of the slow movement's falling sixteenth note groups in the finale. One further element plays an important role: Mozart also renders tribute to Joseph Haydn here with a quotation from his D major quartet op. 50 no. 6, the trio opening of which he uses as beginning of the minuet. The finale itself combines the compositional structure and overall 'tone' of the quartet: here thin- and full-voiced texture articulate the sections, and variously altered recalls play a large part in the concertant structuring. But in addition one can almost see a kind of monothematicism here, drawn from just the first two measures of the theme and by means of which the development and much of the exposition as well show high structural unity and contrapuntal concentration.

Though based on earlier sketches, the B$^\flat$ major quartet KV 589 was finished in May 1790. Between the very concertant layout of the first two movements and the minuet and finale there is a clear expressive gap — what is more, the cello here is hardly a separate soloistic entity. The first movement (*allegro*) is in the same virtuoso-*cantabile* sphere as the D major quartet; indeed, it is clearly related to it with the citation and adoption of the falling sixteenth groups (m. 15 and passim). There are no strong contrasts between both song-like themes, and the development is restricted exclusively to the use of the main theme and forms with it new and harmonically multifaceted episodes, sounding especially rich in changes. The recapitulation is unaltered, while the abbreviated coda takes up elements of the development. The slow movement is another sonata-without-development of considerable extent, occupied mainly by concertant dialogue between first violin and cello; particularly noteworthy here, with the setting aside of the two middle voices, is the care with which the accompaniment flourishes are clearly derived from the thematic material — arabesque and motive are thus inextricably bound with each other. The minuet and, in particular, the trio on the other hand present a kaleidoscope of contrasting forms and characters. In the smallest space are found serenade-like cheerfulness juxtaposed with melancholy sections filled with harsh dissonance, making musical time stand still and abruptly interrupting the playful activity. The finale (with another citation) is connected thematically with the finale theme of Haydn's op. 33 no. 2. It appears at first glance to be an innocent rondo-'last dance;' but a detailed analysis, which space does not allow here, shows an almost adventurous work with harmonic, melodic and rhythmic-metric surprises. Yet its compositional concentration is easily obscured by its pleasant outward characteristics.

The last of Mozart's quartets, KV 590 in F major, also comes from June 1790, and is in almost all formal aspects analogous in structure to its sister work in B$^\flat$ major. Schematically, the first movement is an almost strict sonata movement that achieves its virtuoso transformations solely through the threefold expositions of the main theme: in unison, in changed harmonization, and in concertant gesture. The development is likewise decidedly terse and concentrates on two transformed thematic motives that, in dialogue fashion, are opposed to each other or playfully tossed together without any structural alterations. The coda starts like a second development, but ends rather abruptly with a *grazioso* toss, characterizing well the overall playful character of this movement.

The C major *andante* takes up the rhythm of the slow movement of KV 421, but is otherwise very much its own piece. Notable here is the interconnection of variation and sonata movement: the exposition is easily divided into a group made up of a theme and four variations, there is no secondary theme at all and the brief development carries the various transformation techniques into remote harmonic regions. The minuet is especially interesting on account of its uneven phrases — as in the trio opening of two five measure groups. Yet this irregularity, and many other formal departures in these late quartets, remains a latent factor and not a focal point of the compositional work which is quite definitely oriented toward harmony.

Another multi-layered masterwork analogous to the finale of the B$^\flat$ major quartet KV 589 is the rather *perpetuum · mobile* finale of KV 590, which with its wild counterpoint and expressive oppositions is almost as harmonically untamed as its sister-work. For example the transition to the development, and the gruff juxtaposition of C major and D$^\flat$ major (m. 133/134) are perhaps as uncompromising as other places decried as dissonant in the Haydn quartets.

Next to the young works which adhere closely to models and the self-asserting Haydn quartets, Mozart's "Prussian" quartets constitute a third level in the quartet production of the Salzburg master. This certainly owes nothing to the economic compositional motive which in the summer of 1790, almost a year and a half after the visit to Potsdam, no longer played a role in any case. This third level has an unadorned subjectivity clothed in convention and concertant virtuoso styles. Unlike Haydn, Mozart did not identify himself with the string quartet genre. For him it was not an area of continuous, progressive work, as were his symphonies, piano concertos or even string quintets. For this reason the four late quartets in particular — for all their mastery — do not play the same role in the history of the genre as do Mozart's Haydn quartets, and in the field of set formal structure and fully realized individuality they stand somewhat below the late quartets of Haydn.

Ludwig van Beethoven

"Three quartets were played, one by Haydn, then one by Mozart, and lastly one by Beethoven. It was very interesting for me to observe, in this succession, that each of the three has perfected the genre in keeping with his own personality. Haydn created it from the pure, bright source of his amiable, original nature, ever unique in his naiveté and cheerful good humor. Mozart's richer and more powerful fantasy ranged farther and expressed, in many a movement, the heights and depths of his inner being. He also set more value on skillful craftsmanship, thus building his palace upon Haydn's pleasant-fantastic gardenhouse. Beethoven has already lived in this palace from early on, and so it only remained for him to express his own genius in his own forms, creating that daring proud tower on which no other could set, even lightly, without breaking his neck."[1]

Johann Friedrich Reichard's famous characterization of the three Viennese composers summarizes quite well the attitude of their contemporaries, which attitude — then as today — tended to undervalue Haydn somewhat. But his statements on the role of Beethoven were made at a time when only the op. 18 and op. 59 quartets existed.

1 Johann Friedrich Reichard, *Vertraute Briefe, geschrieben auf einer Reise nach Wien und den österreichischen Staaten zu Ende des Jahres 1808 und zu Anfang 1809*, ed. Gustave Gugitz (Munich, 1915).

In the meantime the literature on Beethoven's string quartets has become so large it is almost impossible to survey.[2] Thus, unlike most other chapters, this discussion must be restricted to Beethoven's string quartets considered solely in the light of the genre's history — indeed, considerations of space preclude any detailed, or in-depth analyses.

Apart from a few contrapuntal studies for strings from the time he was working with Albrechtsberger, there were sixteen string quartets written between 1798 and 1826 and, as was perhaps only true of Haydn up to that point, they span not only the entire creative life of the composer, but also encompass whole stylistic epochs. The op. 18 quartets still clearly depend on the model of Mozart and Haydn; the late quartets from the years 1825/26 on the other hand advance up to the very threshold of 'new music.' They are to such a great extent isolated forerunners of the new that almost the entire nineteenth century — we will get to the exceptions — left a wide, respectful arc around these works. The singular rank as well as the historical import of these quartets was first measured only by composers and music lovers of the early twentieth century.

The six op. 18 string quartets (no. 1 in F major, no. 2 in G major, no. 3 in D major, no. 4 in c minor, no. 5 in A major, no. 6 in B♭ major) were written in the years 1798 and 1799, and were published a year later, in two editions, in parts, of three quartets each. They are dedicated to

2 Only the most important monographs are named here; individual essays are to be found in the bibliography Theodor Helm, *Beethovens Streichquartette* (Leipzig, 1885); Vincent d'Indy, *Cours de Composition musicale* (Paris, 1903), no. 33, vol. 2: "Les seize quatuors de Beethoven" Daniel Gregory Mason, *The quartets of Beethoven* (New York, 1947) Hugo Riemann, *Beethovens Streichquartette* (Berlin, 1910); Philip Radcliffe, *Beethoven's String Quartets* (London, 1965); Ivan Mahaim, *Beethoven. Naissance et Renaissance des Derniers Quatuors* (Paris, 1964), vol. 2; Joseph Kerman, *The Beethoven Quartets* (London, 1967).

Prince Lobkowicz, in whose house quartet soirées regularly took place. It was from these gatherings that the Schuppanzigh quartet evolved as a fixed ensemble. Gustav Nottebohm[3] had shown by means of the dated sketch books that the D major quartet was composed first. The F major work, chronologically in second place, was reworked before publication,[4] for Beethoven, who had already sent a first version to his friend Karl Amenda in 1798, wrote to him shortly after the publication of the quartet: "Don't pass your quartet on any further; I have greatly revised it, since I only now know how to write quartets correctly . . ." Beethoven appears to have learned quartet writing less during his time as a pupil of Haydn than in direct study of his works. One thus knows that he himself also copied for direct study not only the scores of Haydn's C major quartet, but also of Mozart's A major quartet KV 464 from the parts (which were all that had been published at that time). However, "run of the mill" quartet composition in Vienna of the late eighteenth century also had a certain influence: for example the quartets of Ignaz Pleyel, or those by Emanuel Aloys Förster, highly esteemed by Beethoven, also acted as points of compositional orientation.

For Beethoven, thirty years old when the op. 18 quartets were published, the compositional starting point was quite different from that of Haydn, Mozart or Schubert: the one 'created' the genre, the other two wrote numerous quartet compositions in early youth, without any pretension to the individuality they achieved only later in their mature works. Beethoven's op. 18 is most comparable to

3 Gustav Nottebohm, *Beethoveniana* (Leipzig, 1872–1887), vol. 2.

4 Hans Joseph Wedig, *Beethovens Streichquartett op. 18 Nr. 1 und seine erste Fassung* (Bonn, 1922).

the six Haydn quartets of Mozart; it is also the fruit of a "long and difficult labor," with clear borrowings from its models as well as early expressions of those traits later to be identified as typically Beethovenian.

The D major quartet op. 18 no. 3, the earliest and most internally unified quartet of the cycle, represents on a high level and yet without expressly individual character the quartet standard of the late eighteenth century. Here, in an inversion of the phrase coined by Adolf Bernhard Marx, is found "more quartet than Beethoven."

The first movement, *Allegro*, in particular with the episodic role of the secondary theme, is clearly related in formal plan to Haydn's early and middle quartets up to op. 33. It is surprising that the secondary theme enters in C major (instead of A major). The development is quite brief and conventional in its course; unlike 'mature' Beethoven, there are found scarcely any thematic or dynamic contrasts. Developmental work (as is still usual in op. 18) is built upon harmonic transformation or contrapuntal combination. Thematic work, which has almost become paradigmatic in the appreciation of Beethoven's music, is here still rather the exception. A varied, shortened recapitulation (107:80 measures) and a coda that takes up the secondary theme unchanged close this movement, which finds its first contrast in the B$^\flat$ major *andante con moto*. Here Beethoven writes — as quasi lyric center of a generally lyric quartet — a tight, carefully worked sonata movement with occasional *bicinia* voice leading, reminiscent of the slow movements of Mozart's "Prussian" quartets. Here again thematic work appears in contrapuntal forms (measure four of the theme is, in the recall, used as a countersubject in the second violin, and the main theme appears in inversion in the development). The technique of the coda foreshadows the mature formal practice wherein the thematic material is reduced to its melodic and rhythmic fundamentals. While the Scherzo (marked only as *allegro* and with a figurated minor *alternativo*) is rather conventional, the finale is a more comprehensive, fully contrapuntal, finely crafted sonata movement of great technical refinement. Planned in the first sketches as a *perpetuum mobile,* the finale certainly has that *tarantella* quality familiar from the late Schubert quartets. But here it is invested with strict thematic work of such importance that it threatens to overshadow the first movement. The thematic structure, arising more from theoretical planning than from spontaneous melodic inspiration, can be analyzed as follows: the main theme of the last movement is derived from a series of four falling thirds and three rising fourths:

Example 15

The F major quartet op. 18 no. 1, apostrophized by Louis Spohr as a model of string quartet composition, is especially well known on account of its first movement, the main motive of which, probably derived from a development figure in Mozart's string trio KV 563, is a pervasive presence within the texture, similar only to the themes in the piano sonata op. 31 no. 2 and in the fifth symphony op. 67 — these being analogously concise in rhythm. In the Amenda version, this motive was even more insistent than in the printed version; it appears there

130 times, and in the published version only 104. Numerous parallels to op. 18 no. 3 are found in the formal layout. The secondary theme is episodic and remains undeveloped; the recapitulation is abbreviated and the proportions of the sonata movement subsections (exposition 114, development 64, recapitulation 102, coda 35 measures) correspond to each other. The slow movement, *Adagio affettuoso ed appassionato* in d minor and with a rather melodramatic structure, is better explained on emotional than formal grounds. It has been related more than once to the reference to the grave scene from *"Romeo and Juliet"* in an exchange of letters between Beethoven and Amenda. Aria-like and ornamental elements dominate in this sonata movement, which has parallels in the *Largo e mesto* from the piano sonata op. 10 no. 3 and in the trio op. 9 no. 1. Haydn's quartet op. 55 no. 2 should be seen as a model for the formal scheme.[5] Developmental work manifests itself here less as structural dismemberment than as schematic formal contrast of the expressive levels and dynamics.

---

5 Reginald Barrett-Ayres, *Joseph Haydn and the string quartet* (London, 1974), 379.

Example 16

M. 67

The scherzo, related in its layout and aperiodic structure to that of the first symphony op. 21, has a motivically related trio that is strongly periodic in form. But the trio, with its harmonically and formally open end leads cogently back to the scherzo. The finale, a sonata-rondo with contrapuntal development elements, does not attain the constructive artistry of the first two movements. Thus the state of advancement of the genre can be seen in op. 18 primarily in the unevenness of the movements within a quartet.

The G major quartet op. 18 no. 2, with its retrospective traits — almost quotations — is rightly considered Beethoven's *"hommage à Haydn,"* just as the A major quartet op. 18 no. 5 is *"hommage à Mozart."* Both works are simpler than their forerunners, formally as well as harmonically. In them Beethoven took pains — also clearly revealing the connection to their respective models — to produce a characteristic unity throughout the quartets, refraining from the occasional ground-breaking dimensions and constructive pretensions of any one movement in favor of cyclic connection and a single character embracing all the individual movements. This intention is particularly apparent in the layout of the slow movements, which are rather brief and formally transparent. For the G major quartet Haydn's quartets op. 33 no. 5 and op. 76 no. 1 have been referred to specifically as models:[6] formal details from the E^b major quartet op. 33 no. 2 may also have been influential. The firm basis in tradition is a formal 'relief,' in turn setting free structural powers in matters of detail that were perhaps suppressed in a very stylistically secure handling of contrapuntal techniques (in the development of the first movement) as well as

6 Barrett-Ayres, *op. cit.,* 380; Kerman, *loc. cit.,* 45ff.

in the rather concertant-virtuoso type of voice leading. Above all the middle part of the slow movement merits special notice: an *adagio cantabile* in which Beethoven creates a dance-piece parody — a hint at the finale of op. 18 no. 6, but also at the *Alla tedesca* in the op. 130 string quartet. Cyclic interconnection of the individual movements is especially remarkable in the theme of the finale (a dialoguing sonata-rondo) derived from traditional ideas in the first movement.

While the traditional borrowings from Haydn are more a matter of the 'tone' and idiomatic style, the borrowings from Mozart in the A major quartet op. 18 no. 5 clearly go much farther: the model here — for all four movements — is Mozart's A major quartet KV 464, the most "intensely crafted" of the cycle of Haydn quartets. In addition, the definitely lightweight first movement as well as the second — an almost archaically charming minuet (!) — align closely with the model, and both last movements correspond not only in formal layout and timbral character, but also in the second theme of the last movement. The *Andante cantabile,* a variation movement with five figurative variations and a well defined development section, can be traced beyond Mozart: the model for Mozart's movement was surely the slow movement of Haydn's string quartet in D major op. 20 no. 4.[7] The last movement, which in balance between constructive craft and relaxed playfulness (certainly, in the conventional sense, the most successful last movement of the cycle) is reminiscent of the finale of the "Prague" symphony, KV 504.

The c minor quartet op. 18 no. 4 has been criticized on stylistic grounds particularly by Hugo Riemann. On account of the lack of sketches in the op. 18 sketch

7 Kerman, *loc. cit.,* 59—61.

collection, Riemann has assigned it an earlier date of origin, basing this also on a comparison with the E$^{\flat}$ major duet for viola and cello, probably from the Bonn period. Yet if one relates this quartet (which in its place within the work cycle follows the convention valid since Haydn's a minor quartet op. 9) to other c minor works of the later 90's, in particular the piano sonata op. 13 and the string trio op. 9 no. 2, that cliché of a rhetorical-pathetic minor character can be clearly seen, with frequent use of figures from the repertoire of *Affektenlehre*. Indeed, one therefore need not establish an early time of origin in order to state that Beethoven has here adhered in form and character to tradition. The simplification of formal elements and their interrelationship is continued in the terse construction of the first movement as well as in the finale, a clearly constructed virtuoso rondo entirely without developmental elements — quite primitive as opposed to the rondo of op. 18 no. 5. In confronting the problem of the slow movement. Beethoven here attempted to work with a mixed form: as expressive contrast to the rather uniformly dramatic first movement there appears a playful *Andante scherzoso quasi Allegretto*, in which the sonata form with fugal opening is laid out analogously to the slow movements of the piano sonata op. 10 no. 2 and the first symphony op. 21, but with a tendency toward that kind of 'mechanical' motion, somewhat akin to the slow movement of the eighth symphony op. 93.

The last of the early quartets, op. 18 no. 6 in B$^{\flat}$ major, is a close neighbor in the sketchbooks to the piano sonata op. 22. The relationship is indicated not only by the key parallel, but also by formal and thematic details. The dominance of compositional proportion can be seen especially in the first movement, so precisely constructed that it can do without a coda, and the three parts of which —

exposition (90 measures), development (83 measures) and recapitulation (90 measures) — correspond perfectly. Comparable to the frequently obvious model of Haydn's op. 76 no. 4, the development is dissociative and fragmentarily rhetorical rather than goal-oriented. There are also extended contrapuntal sections (development, m. 112—137) and a wide ranging field of thematic reduction (m. 150—175). The slow movement, composed of three clear parts and almost rococo ornamental work, and the scherzo, with numerous hemiolic forms, are formally secure, but scarcely tower over the comparable movements of the other works. Only the last movement is unusual in its uncommon combination of slow and fast sections, not sequenced as in op. 18 no. 2 but rather interwoven in many ways. the slow section, provided by Beethoven with the superscript *"La Malinconia,"*[8] harmonically far outpaces anything comparable of that time and, after a rather static montage at the beginning (not restricted to the function of slow introduction but rather appearing twice as contrast as well as connective — an abbreviated reminiscence within the two fast parts) runs a regular course, somewhat similarly to op. 131. Neither in Haydn's nor in Mozart's quartets is an analogous spot found; the most comparable appears to me to be the first movement of Haydn's E♭ major symphony Hob. I/103; there the slow introduction has neither the complexity nor the extent, but the contrast between slow introduction and fast main section is equally sharp and forms that kind of unbridgeable expressive contrast, with a *perpetuum mobile* and quite frivolously primitive *alla Tedesca-allegretto* opposed

8 On Beethoven's string quartet op. 18 no. 6 and in particular on *"La Malinconia"* there will shortly appear in the collection "Beethoven" (*Wege der Forschung* vol. 428; Darmstadt, in preparation) edited by Ludwig Finscher, two contributions by Carl Dahlhaus and Arno Forschert. The manuscript has been made available to me by the editor, but it cannot be dealt with here.

to the harmonic labyrinth of the *adagio*. The climax of the final movement, reached in op. 18 no. 5 through structural intensity, is achieved here by yoking together of the incompatible, in the rupture of conventional form — not structurally, but legitimized by its expressive fantasy.

Five years lie between the completion of the op. 18 quartet cycle and those written next, the "Rasumovsky" quartets op. 59, and thus stylistic worlds separate the new works from the old; there are "peculiarities of style which made the understanding of the works uncommonly difficult to contemporaries (. . .): the expansively 'symphonic' tone, contradicting the generic canon developed from the Haydn tradition of the classic string quartet (which Beethoven's op. 18 still largely followed), and which manifests itself in the extent of the movements and of the whole cycle of movements, in the sheer mass of sound, in the delineation of an extremely wide range, in the orchestral use of elements such as range, tone color, harmony and rhythm. There are also the technical demands on the first violin above all, into which — quite (and not by chance) as in the contemporary violin concerto — much of the French "Viotti" school and (a further example of the turn from the classical quartet traditions and norms) elements of the *quator brillant* indirectly find their way. One sees also the replacement of familiar classical theme types with arching *cantabile* melodies (. . .) with wide-ranging consequences: the general displacement of classical thematic work, for which such melodies appear scarcely suitable, through techniques of variative and *'Fortspinnung'* development and linear voice leading."[9] Joseph Kerman[10] rightly names his chapter

9 Ludwig Finscher, "Beethovens Streichquartett op. 59,3" in Gerhard Schuhmacher, ed., *Zur Musikalischen Analyse* (*WdF* vol. 262; Darmstadt, 1974), 122—160, specifically p. 123f.

10 Kerman, *loc. cit.*, 89—154.

on the Rasumovsky quartets "After the Eroica," and for the evolution of the genre in the Beethovenian oeuvre as well as for its evolution overall, the op. 59 quartets (in particular the F major quartet op. 59 no. 1) played the very same role as his symphony in F major op. 55 did for the evolution of the symphony.

The three op. 59 quartets commissioned by the Russian ambassador Count Andreas Rasumovsky, were composed in the years 1805/06; and they were, as the sketches show,[11] written in the sequence as published at the beginning of 1808 by Tobias Haslinger in Vienna.

What differentiates these quartets from their antecendents (even beyond the factors named by Ludwig Finscher) is the increased individualization in the F major quartet, which, with exchange of the inner movements, does indeed keep to the traditional four movement scheme. But at the same time all four movements are constructed of an irregular, experimental type of sonata form: the first movement does not repeat the exposition, the development achieves considerable predominance as opposed to the exposition and recapitulation, while the coda has almost the character of a second, expansive development (measure proportions 102:150:93:52). A clearly laid out, rather lyric (though departing from the movement's character) main theme opens the movement in the cello, and is repeated by the violin in an at times tonally unstable dominant area. A cadential confirmation of the fundamental key of F major is first found in measures 18/19.

11 Cf. Gustav Nottebohm, *Zweite Beethoveniana* (Leipzig, 1887), 79ff.

Example 17

mf .e dolce

Thematic work in the traditional sense is found mostly between sections and in transitions during the exposition, at times built of main theme material. The actual development presents very little motivic disintegration or thematic contrast, mainly on account of melodic similarity, which in these themes can almost be thought of as variative transformational forms of a hidden 'Ur-theme,' making them unsuitable for such motivic breaking down. If one sought to describe this new kind of developmental work, appearing in clearly demarcated sections (m. 103—143; m. 144—175; m. 176—218; m. 219—253), one could speak of 'character variations' of the main theme, with which each of these four sections begins: contrapuntal-thematic opposition in the first, harmonic-concertant transformations in the second, strict, almost 'scholastic' counterpoint with a real double fugue in the third, and a harmonically figurative area of resolution with anticipation of the recapitulation in the fourth part. The recapitulation is abbreviated and leads quickly — after its true beginning — into a harmonic area not yet touched on, where half and whole step relationships almost outweigh those of the traditional fifth and third. The coda first brings this process to its full unfolding, presenting the main theme in its previous characterization.

The second movement *Allegretto vivace e sempre scherzando"* is still more unusual than the first. It represents the dance movement by its placement in the cycle, yet its static five section shape (in op. 59 five part form dominates the scherzos with twice recalled principle of sonata form, though it doesn't meet the tonal requirements. In all, nine independent (but at the same time interrelated) motives are almost kaleidoscopically connected, exchanged and combined; thematic reduction to the simplest material, here on an intricate ground thythm

Example 18

♫♩ | ♫♩ | ♫♫♫ | ♩. |

is balanced through a formal synthesis, comparable only with the scherzi from the middle Mahler symphonies, particularly in their 'incompatibility' in relationship of material and elaboration. The slow movement *Adagio e mesto,* one of the few minor movements in major works by Beethoven, plays with its main theme on the Baroque "hymn or pathos type"[12] and has thematic parallels with the slow movement of Haydn's string quartet op. 64 no. 3.[13] Here — and indeed at its most conventional in the quartets — is a sonata movement with its *quasi* 'cited' expressive gesture. The relationship with the *adagio* of the F major quartet op. 18 no. 1 is apparent, and here extramusical associations especially appear to determine the compositional type. The finale, in which Beethoven (as in the trio from op. 59 no. 2) has used a *"Thème*

---

12 Cf. Warren Kirkendale, *Fuge und Fugato in der Kammermusik des Rokoko und der Klassik* (Tutzing, 1966), 137 and Finscher, *loc. cit.,* 125.

13 Here Ludwig Finscher (*loc. cit.,* 125, note 10) cites op. 64,2, apparently a misprint.

14 Kerman, *loc. cit.,* 110.

russe,"[15] is also in sonata form, yet- this is somewhat forced upon the folky theme more suited to a rondo form. But the technical mastery is such that no contradiction of material and elaboration is apparent. The relation to the first movement — especially in the main theme — is so clear that the presumption that the finale presents commentary or parody[16] of the first movement cannot be excluded. The irregularity of this sonata movement, working once again far more with character variations and counterpoint than with traditional development, is seen as much in the proportions of the movement sections (99:76:85:64) as in the subdominant (B$^\flat$ major) entry of the recapitulation. In addition, for the transition into the development Beethoven uses exactly this same violin figure that leads from the coda of the slow movement immediately into the finale (cf. *Adagio* m. 130—132/*Allegro* m. 92/98).[17]

If one considers the quartet in its entirety, it appears "unusual also as to the manner and way in which expressive characters of the movements relate to each other. Thus the outer movements appear ambivalent in the sense that they are firmly identified neither through performance indications nor through allusions to traditional expressive types. The middle movements, with *scherzando* character on the one hand and pathetic-*lamento* character on the other, form the sharpest imaginable expressive opposition."[18]

The e minor quartet op. 59 no. 2 creates a perfect

15 Walter Salmen, "Zur Gestaltung der *'Thèmes russes'* in Beethovens opus 59" in *Festschrift Walter Wiora* (Kassel, 1967), 397—404.

16 Kerman, *loc. cit.,* 112.

17 Kerman, *loc. cit.,* 114.

18 Finscher, *loc. cit.,* 126.

contrast in almost all aspects: it is very much shorter, clearer in form, far more involved with the relationship of the movements than with individuality and progressiveness.[19] The *Allegro* opens with a (thematically significant) 'curtain raiser' as known from numerous quartets of Joseph Haydn,[20] that shows intensive harmonic and motivic work. The harmonic motto of the beginning already contains the melodic fifth that dominates the main theme.

Example 19

The proportions of the movements correspond almost completely (71:69:71:46 measures) just as in op. 18 no. 5; exposition and recapitulation and (even more clearly) development and coda are almost identical in their beginnings. Symmetrical relationships characterize this movement to such an extent that Kerman's explanations for the instruction (probably the last in the history of the genre) to repeat the second half, that is, the development and recapitulation, is immediately obvious: first of all, with this repetition the symmetrical relationships within the movement correspond and a balance is struck with the following slow movement.[21] The development — although

19 Kerman, *loc. cit.*, 119: "But the e minor quartet is ready to check the full elaboration of the single movements in view of the integrity of the whole."

20 Cf. Haydn, quartet op. 71 no. 1 and 3; op. 76 no. 1.

21 Kerman, *loc. cit.*, 121.

mostly adhering to traditional thematic work as in the F major quartet op. 59 no. 1, is just as irregular. In the F major work it is the contrapuntal writing that breaks away from the formal canon; here it is the dramatic gesture, the harmonic half step succession that functions theatrically, as does the inserted citation from the exposition (m. 115—121) and the obscuring of the recapitulation entry by means of dovetailing, and through the filling out of the structurally important rest (m. 142—143). The coda, with the appearance of a second development and fadeaway ending, also has a dramatic-gestural tinge. And finally, the harmonic filling out of the half step by means of the Neapolitan sixth chord is a genuine theatrical device, which Beethoven in the contemporary first version of his opera *Leonora* (1805) used in many instances (in the new version of 1814 these are largely expunged). The slow movement, here in the traditional second place, is in E major, thus reversing the tonal relationship with regard to change of mode, in connection with the F major quartet. It bears the indication *Molto Adagio. Si tratta questo pezzo con molto di sentimento,* and the hymn or chorale-like 'tone' of the movement, a type modeled in numerous late Haydn quartets,[22] already early on evoked an association with the transcendental. Czerny left an anecdote that this *adagio* was an inspiration that came to Beethoven as he looked up at the star-strewn heavens and pondered the harmony of the spheres.[23] What is certainly valid regarding this association is the contemplative, rather static character (as opposed to sonata form) with scarcely any well directed thematic work. In its place appear motivic recombina-

---

22 Haydn, quartets op. 71 no. 2; op. 76 no. 1 op. 76 no. 5; op. 77 no. 1.

23 Thayer-Deiters-Riemann, *Ludwig van Beethovens Leben,* vol. 2 (Leipzig, 1922), 523.

tions and the ever new clothing of the main theme with figuratively varied accompaniment elements. This tendency toward the "never ending,"[24] reinforced by an extremely slow tempo and the modal beginning of the main theme, points the way to the *"heiligen Dankgesang"* in the a minor quartet, op. 132.

The scherzo, as in the two other op. 59 quartets, is in five parts with the form A B A B A and also combines e minor and E major (as does the whole work in any case). This is a unique instance among Beethoven's works — contrast based solely on the modal distinction. The scherzo is built on a one measure syncopated motive, a type later used by Brahms. The modulations using the Neapolitan sixth chord are reminiscent of the first movement. In the *"Maggiore"* trio Beethoven uses the *"Thème russe,"* a six measure melody (that appears once again in the coronation scene of Mussorgski's *"Boris Godunov"*) in the form of a strict fugue, which with fourfold voice entry proceeds in real three part counterpoint, and which culminates in voice pairing and stretto — first in the original phrasing, then *legato.*

Example 20

24 Kerman, *loc. cit.*, 129. Consider the striking melodic analogy between the *Adagio* and the *"Benedictus"* of the *Missa Solemnis.* Warren Kirkendale. "Beethovens *Missa solemnis* und die rhetorische Tradition" in *Sitzungsberichte der Österreichischen Akademie der Wissenschaften*, Philosophisch-historische Klasse, 271, vo. 1971, 145f.

The *presto* finale, a clearly formed rondo, has that sprightly character as found in the finales of Haydn's mature quartets. It achieves an almost symphonic expression with frequent use of *basso ostinato* and clear separation of melody and accompaniment. Indeed, Beethoven quotes no *"thème russe"* here, but the 'tone' of the main theme, which begins in C major and first cadences to e minor (the fundamental key of the movement) after eight measures, and of the accompaniment as well has something folky about it; Kerman concurs: ". . . sometimes one can hear the triangle, bass drum, and piccolo of the Turkish band."[25] The "obsessive rhythmic drive"[26] of the main theme that appears at the beginning four times in succession characterizes the entire movement, while the secondary theme remains largely episodic. Integration and cyclic connection are found especially in the closing part of the exposition, where the interlacing three note groups and the frequent use of the Neapolitan sixth chord remind one of the closing part of the *"Maggiore."* As in the finale of the F major quartet Beethoven writes into the development of the movement a double fugato which "through the rhythmic form of the themes (even eighth note motion against even halves) creates the appearance of an exercise in formal counterpoint after Fux and Albrechtsberger, but much less archaic in its melodic theme."[27] The reprise of the secondary theme (m. 216—246) is integrated into the development and is missing from its logical place in the abbreviated recapitulation (m. 275—342). The three part coda makes two starts with the transitional figure, stops —

25 Kerman, *loc. cit.*, 130.

26 Kerman, *loc. cit.*, 133.

27 Finscher, *loc. cit.*, 132f.

before a general pause — on a Neapolitan sixth chord, then cites the main theme and ends in an accelerating, wide ranging cadence in e minor (which key plays a relatively small role within the movement).

"The contrast between the first and second quartet (the contrast between individualization and cyclic linking, W. K.) rises to a new level in the third and final work, not so much with a 'synthesis' of what has gone before but rather in a very complicated way, as is measured in the many-layered connections among the works. Tonal plan and succession of movements are conventional at first glance, but in their correspondences and contrasts refer very pointedly to a relationship with the two other quartets."[28]

The first movement, *Allegro vivace*, begins with a double introduction: first, a tonally unstable slow introduction exhibiting the 'continual' thematic approach proceeds in the chromatic cello line to a low B^b [29] (no longer available on the instrument), greatly expanding the narrow range of the opening, only to close it back up immediately; second, a two part solo cadenza for the first violin. The cadence to the tonic C major at the end of the slow introduction suggests the main theme beginning, yet the C major chord is *quasi* 'reversed' in function through the melodic and metric upbeat. The emphasized dominant seventh chord appears to be the fundamental

28 Finscher, *loc. cit.*, 129. Here thanks are very much due to Ludwig Finscher's analysis of op. 59 no. 3, which has provided the author with numerous important insights, not only for the present description of the C major quartet, but also for all of op. 59.

29 Cf. Finscher, *loc. cit.*, 136—139; Kerman, *loc. cit.*, 134—137, and Peter Gülke, "Introduktion als Widerspruch im System. Zur Dialektik von Thema und Prozessualität bei Beethoven" in *Deutsches Jahrbuch für Musikwissenschat (Peters Jahrbuch)* 1969 (Leipzig , 1970), 19—23.

key. It is only after a repetition on the harmonic areas d minor/A major and a chromatically expanded cadence in measure 43 that the tonic of the work appears and the main theme of the sonata movement enters.

The slow introduction, unique among the movements of op. 59, reminds one in its harmonic daring of the slow introduction to Mozart's C major quartet KV 465.[30] In the main section of the movement Beethoven supports this association through an undisguised citation from the first movement of Mozart's work.[31]

In contrast to the free form of the introduction, the main theme is quite concise and compact. Most notable is the concertant element that in Beethoven's lifetime made this quartet so popular (as opposed to its two sister works). Indeed, concertant elements already appeared tentatively in the introduction. "The thematically, melodically and rhythmically formless circumscription of range and tonality is followed by melodically and rhythmically pointed soloistic gesture that is almost a solo 'cadenza' in the sense of the concerto."[32] The transitional sections are extended in the exposition, which shows concentrated motivic-thematic work and, indeed, refers to the second motive of the 'cadenza' opening throughout. A secondary theme is, however, scarcely elaborated; a series of motives (m. 81ff.) seems to take its place, creating something other than a simple thematic form. The final section consists of a terse fugato. Ludwig Finscher characterizes the importance of the exposition (as opposed to which the development proceeds rather briefly and simply) by

30 Finscher, *loc. cit.*, 136.

31 Cp. mm. 89−90 corresponding to Mozart, KV 465, first movement, mm. 88−91; even more clearly mm. 208−211.

32 Finscher, *loc. cit.*, 138.

its function: "concertant looseness of structure on the one hand, technically artful structure on many levels up to the fugato on the other (and both in many gradations) join with the 'composing out' of the tonal space, toward the interpenetration of motivic solidity and solo cadenza rhapsody, emphatic arrival and retreat of strongly punctuated cadences on the tonic or dominant, dominated by elements of the introduction and first main section."[33]

The development is most notable for its concentration (after the Haydn model) on the elaboration of the second motive, starting from the renewed solo cadenza of the first violin, over the 'mediating interval' of the fifth (m. 118f.) through the reduction to tone repetition (cello m. 127ff.), broadening out to the octave (m. 150ff.), and to the figurative dissolution into cadenza trill of the first violin (m. 173ff.). The abbreviated recapitulation (m. 191 −251) is another − this time very much more extended − violin cadenza with renewed chromatic approach to the tonic. The terse coda concentrates on renewed emphatic cadencing and circumscribes "the basic elements of the movement: cadence emphasis and formal clarity, (apparent) isolation and synthesis of the parameters, motivic concentration and development with changing thematic work, and emphatic traversal of the limits of the range."[34]

The slow movement, *Andante con moto quasi Allegretto* in a minor, consists formally of a combination of sonata movement and song forms, and contrasts with the first movement in several ways. The almost abstract layout is opposed to a very melodious flow that is most clear in the reappearance of the second motive, which here (never in

33 Finscher, *loc. cit.,* 142.

34 Finscher, *loc. cit.,* 146.

the first movement) is connected to the gestural 'sigh' motive. The elegaic tone, evoked by the turning figure of the main theme, is broken up in the movement's episodes, which have a concertant as well as a loose, dancelike character and are reminiscent in their range (compare for instance m. 48—50, m. 127—131) of the first movement while they also anticipate the minuet. This third movement is a *Menuetto grazioso*. In the same sense in which the first movement is the 'model' of a constructive sonata movement, and the second presents that kind of songlike slow movement, this third movement is a model of the archaic-*galante* minuet (to the melodic, *cantabile* character of which the trio, with its climbing triad fanfare strongly contrasts). Especially remarkable here is the coda, which takes up the minuet theme, turns it to minor, leads through a harmonic labyrinth of gliding chord changes and finally ends 'open' on the dominant seventh chord. The finale should — as in the F major quartet op. 59 no. 1 — follow *attacca*. There is a thematic relationship not only between the dancelike episodes of the slow movement and the main theme of the minuet, but also between this and the finale theme — as the following excerpt shows:

Example 21

The *Allegro molto* that closes this work and the cycle has an appropriately double finale function, fulfilled on several levels. "First of all, it functions as the culmination, and therefore has power and moving energy as a closing, emphasized through the minuet coda's function as a slow introduction, and takes on something of a *perpetuum mobile* character with its almost uninterrupted eighth note motion. In the second place, it is a finale because in it the contrapuntal technique of both the other quartets is enormously enlarged upon."[35] Formally, the movement is ambivalent — Ludwig Finscher characterizes it as a "sonata movement, which certainly behaves like a fugue."[36] It begins with a fugue exposition in the dominant, the 'countersubject' of which is reduced after fifteen measures to chordal quarter note and then later half note accompaniment. The tonic is first reached after 46 measures and, through the dominant of the dominant (on which a second theme is motivically derived from the continual succession of eighths), leads to the development, where contrapuntal display and motivic form are proportioned in parodistic figuration. The development, as extensive as the exposition, is clearly separated from a regular recapitulation that begins with a double fugato, and a twice climaxing coda that is larger than the development, with a contrapuntal intensity increasing as it brings the movement in stretto fashion to its emphatic, virtuosic 'crowning conclusion.'

The op. 59 quartets for the most part both perplexed and disoriented contemporaries. At best, the C major quartet could succeed when the listener oriented himself

---

35 Finscher, *loc. cit.,* 151ff.

36 Finscher, *loc. cit.,* 151.

to the virtuoso brilliance of the finale (thereby largely missing the work's intention). Beethoven consequently reacted to this problem in his own manner: in the following sixteen years only two singly published quartets were written and both attained — in different ways — a confirmed place with the public. "The E^b major quartet is an open, unproblematic, clearly consolidated work, like some others written at this time. The f minor quartet is an involved, impassioned, highly idiosyncratic piece, problematic in every one of its movements, advanced in a hundred ways."[37] The E^b major quartet op. 74, composed in 1809, a close contemporary to the sixth symphony, the A major cello sonata, the fifth piano concerto op. 73, and the trio op. 70 no. 2 (the latter two likewise E^b major works) is an appealingly uncomplicated work with concertant traits and was quickly beloved. It is no accident that E^b major is also the key of such related works as the op. 3 string trio and the op. 20 septet. The *Poco adagio* introduction of the first movement — with a tonally clear 'question' motive and the chromatically intensified transition to the *Allegro*-lines up with the tradition of slow introductions; it has nothing of the formal and harmonic frankness of the C major quartet op. 59 no. 3. The first movement, with its opening motive based on a triad arpeggio and the *cantabile* main theme firmly in the subdominant, has something Mozartean about it. In the development and the coda (which takes on the function of a second development: measure relationships 53:61:65:59) an improvisatory element dominates, based far more in timbre and color than in thematic work. The extent of the development can be traced more to *quasi* 'static' fields of resolution (m. 109—124, m. 125—138) than to intensive modulatory work. In

37 Kerman, *loc. cit.*, 156.

any case experimental traits in this work appear for the most part in the area of timbre and tone color. The heavy use of pizzicato (disproportionate for the time) earned the nickname 'harp quartet' for the work, and the virtuoso-concertant violin solo in the coda reminds one of the style of the *quatuor concertant* that evolved in France.

The slow movement, *Adagio ma non troppo* in A♭ major, is as simple and clear as the first movement. The main theme, one of the most beautiful lyric inspirations of the composer (in a creative period rich in melodic invention) is varied three times; in between are inserted rather long, thematically altered episodes depending chiefly on the major-minor exchange — as in the mature quartets of Haydn. The scherzo, marked only as *presto,* has, in its five parts (with coda bridging to the finale) and its key of c minor, clear parallels to the scherzo of the fifth symphony op. 67 as well as to the rhythmic 'drive' and the contrapuntal style of the trio. But unlike the symphony, the scherzo does not proceed into a hymnlike, pathos-filled finale, but rather into a decidedly lightweight variation movement, comparable to the variations in the op. 96 violin sonata from the same period, or the op. 77 piano fantasy. The six variations hold strongly throughout to the structure of the previous theme, figuratively, harmonically and in extent, but clearly alternate in dynamics. Variations 1, 3 and 5 are marked as *sempre forte,* and the variations 2, 4 and 6 as *sempre dolce e piano*. A coda develops the motive of the sixth variation further and ends with an E♭ major cadence intensified in stretto fashion. The character of the quartet, rather more improvisatory than 'worked out', and the clear emphasis on timbral and coloristic aspects may have contributed to the fact that this quartet had an immediate influence on

127

the generation of the 'Romantic' quartet composers; such influences are found in Schubert's c minor movement D. 820 and in his G major quartet op. 161 (scherzo) as well as in Mendelssohn's E^b major quartet op. 12.

The vast difference between the E^b major and the f minor quartet is already reflected in the dedication. The earlier one, like the op. 18 quartet, was dedicated to the princely patron Lobkowicz, who a year before, jointly with Rasumovsky and archduke Rudolph von Hapsburg, had bequeathed a yearly salary on Beethoven. The later one, composed in October 1810 under the pall of Beethoven's failed marriage plans, and first published in 1816, was dedicated to his closest friend, the court secretary Nikolaus Zmeskall von Domanovec. Beethoven originally had considered leaving the work unpublished — a circumstance that may very likely be traced to its 'avant garde' nature.

"It is in almost every respect at the opposite pole from the playful lightheartedness of the E^b major work: gloomy and introverted, as gruff in thematic work as in timbral aspect and of a formal and technical concentration that immediately points to the late quartets."[38] Rhetorical elements in the music are forsaken, especially transitional and closing sections. "In the Rasumovsky quartets he labored to individualize such passages. In the E^b major quartet he enjoyed stylizing them. Now he simply does without them."[39] The first movement, *Allegro con brio,* presents at the beginning two brief and contrasting motivic inspirations: an expanded turn figure presented in unison, and a dotted octave leap counter-

38 Ludwig Finscher, "Beethoven. Die mittlere Quartette." Notes accompanying the cassette by the Vegh Quartet, Telefunken SPA 25096, p. 4 (German release).

39 Kerman, *loc. cit.,* 4.

pointed with upbeat figures. There is added a lyrical twelve measure passage (built harmonically on the tritone c–g$\flat$) that functions as contrast. To this, finally, is added the three measure version of the main motive, on which (m. 24) the secondary theme in A major is superimposed. The closing part of the exposition, which already has a developmental character, is based on ostinato excerpts derived from the sixteenth note motion of the beginning. The development, here comprising 22 measures, continues this thematic work and intensifies it harmonically, sharply contrasting the areas around the fundamental tones f/g$\flat$, c/d$\flat$ (measure proportions 59:22:47:23). The recapitulation is obviously shortened in the main theme group (it lacks measures 1–17 of the exposition) but is expanded developmentally in the secondary theme area. The coda continues the reduction and contraposting techniques where the component parts of the main theme are placed in opposition in outer or middle voices (m. 138ff.).

The slow movement, *Allegretto ma non troppo,* is in D major. Before this, such unifying tonal strategy was found in this creative period at its most extreme in the E$\flat$ major/ B major succession in the op. 73 piano concerto or in the op. 77 piano fantasy. The basis here is a bridge form (A B B A' Coda), in which homophonic and polyphonic principles are opposed to each other and, through the introductory cello phrase (which also takes on a bridge function: m. 64–75), interchanged with the contrasting themes presented at the beginning. The *cantabile*-elegaic main theme and the increasingly chromatic fugue theme are counterpointed with each other (m. 143ff.). The harmonic intensity of the first movement (in particular the tritone interval) is here increased; the major tonality, untroubled at the beginning, is ever more overshadowed through chromaticization and thus subsequently negated.

Therefore the *Allegretto* (as has also been shown by Joseph Kerman in a detailed analysis[40]) is an actualization of the problem already exposed in the slow movement of op. 59 no. 3, just as the first movement harks back to the e minor quartet.

Beethoven superscribed the third movement with the tempo marking *Allegro Assai vivace ma serioso*. Scarcely a scherzo, it is much more a scurrying, syncopated march of that gloomy-threatening character as appeared a little later with Berlioz, Liszt, or, ultimately, with Mahler — a *'Totentanz'* analogous to the conventional scherzo — and also a foreshadowing of the *Alla Marcia* in the a minor quartet op. 132. Set in opposition to the rhythmically concentrated, clearly articulated f minor main section is a rather chorale-like trio in double copy in which the keys G♯ major/D major and C major, counterpointed by running violin figurations, make the harmonic connection, mediated by the Neapolitan sixth chord and seventh chord, taking up the tritone and semitone of the first two movements. The finale, reaching back to the *'lamento'* character of the slow movement and thereby separating the main section from the rhythmic intensity of the march, begins with an eight measure introduction, *Larghetto espressivo* — probably the most conventional part of the quartet. The main section, with the self-contradictory marking *Allegretto agitato,* is a mixture of rondo and sonata form. More important nevertheless than this rather loosely handled compositional structure is the change from the traditionally lightweight 6/8 *allegretto* type to a hurried, abrupt, strongly thematic movement which, with its laconic manner and the renunciation of all things episodic or virtuosic is diametrically opposed to

40 Kerman, *loc. cit.,* 176—180.

the conventional finale character. In particular the 'second theme' of running scales in dynamic alternation of *f* and *p* over middle voice sixteenths contradicts that finale 'looseness' (m. 32ff.; m. 82ff.). The movement appears — reaching back in the first violin for the series of tones d-d♭ -g that already dominates the other movements — to die out *ppp*. But then Beethoven delivers the final gesture again: "a fantastic evocation of an opera buffa finale"[41] in F major, but melodically chromaticized and strengthened through contrapuntal techniques. As in the finale of the B♭ major quartet op. 18 no. 6, the close here is definitely unorganic, as if 'stuck on.' The F major stretto, "precisely through its very express lack of relationship to everything that went before, denies the resolution of the major mode 'brightening.' The expressive realm of the late quartets, in which the traditions of the genre survive only in total metamorphosis or as the ruins of its former cohesion, begins to become visible."[42]

"Ripeness in the late works of Beethoven the renowned composer is not comparable to the ripeness of fruit. His mature productions are not commonly round, but rather furrowed and quite torn apart. They bear no sweetness, are thorny and shrivelled, tart to ordinary taste. There is lacking in them all the harmony that the classical esthetic of the art work was accustomed to, and instead show the path away from, rather than growth out of, history. The usual view tries to clear it up thus, that they are products of the reckless self-probing subjectivity (. . .) in which (since for the sake of self expression the perimeter of the form might be broken) harmony turns to the dissonance of its passion, and sensual charm is disdained by

41 Kerman, *loc. cit.*, 182.

42 Finscher, *loc. cit.* (see note 37), 4.

virtue of the self domination of the liberated soul."[43] The beginning of an essay of Theodor W. Adorno on the 'late style of Beethoven' gives the grounds for difficulties of appreciation faced by contemporaries (though the hearers increased in number after Beethoven's death) in the last five quartets of Beethoven — those op. 127 to 135 quartets, arising in close sequence, sometimes even parallel with each other after a hiatus of more than twelve years in this genre. They bring to a close Beethoven's late works, introduced with the *Missa solemnis,* the ninth symphony and the late piano sonatas.

Beethoven's renewed interest in this genre is, in the opinion of Schindler, often ascribed to extra-musical reasons in the traditional Beethoven literature, that is, with the commission of the Russian Prince Nikolaus Galitzin of November 1822, and with the return of Ignaz Schuppanzigh to Vienna in the spring of 1823. Both occasions certainly lent support to the project, but a written offer to the publisher Peters from the spring of 1822 shows that Beethoven was already working with quartet composition again. The internal, and more important, basis ought therefore to have been recorded: that it occurred to Beethoven to draw a sum — to compose out what was yet unsaid in those genres that were important to him and that were highly esteemed in the esthetic of the time in the symphony, the piano sonata and the string quartet.

The five string quartets, together with the separately published *Grosse Fuge* and later composed finale op. 130, which comprise the work group of 'late quartets,' arose between the spring of 1822 and November 1826, but certainly not in the sequence that the opus numbers suggest.

43 Theodor W. Adorno, *Spätstil Beethovens,* quoted from Adorno, *Moments musicaux. Neu gedruckte Aufsätze 1928—1964* (Frankfurt, 1964), 13.

For the fairly exact datings we are particularly indebted to the researches of Ivan Mahaim.[44] According to him, the E♭ major quartet op. 127 (that work optimistically said to be near completion in the letter to Peters) was written between the spring of 1822 and the end of 1824. It was first performed on March 6, 1825 in Vienna by the Schuppanzigh quartet and was published with a dedication to Prince Galitzin in June 1826 by Schott in Mainz. This quartet also thoroughly disproves the reputation of a contemporary lack of interest: it was — again according to the researches of Mahaim — performed with great success a total of six times in Vienna within two months.[45]

The next work was the op. 132 quartet in a minor on which Beethoven worked from the summer of 1824 to the end of July 1825. It was first performed on the sixth of November 1825, likewise by the Schuppanzigh quartet and was published, also dedicated to Prince Galitzin, in September 1827 by Schlesinger in Paris. The B♭ major op. 130, in the original version with the *Grosse Fuge* as its closing movement, was finished at the beginning of November 1825 and at its first performance on March 21, 1826 the second and the fourth movement were encored — certainly also no indication of a 'failure.' It was published (in the revised version with the subsequently composed last movement) in May 1827 by Artaria and is likewise dedicated to Galtzin; a score edition in the original version was first obtained in 1953 by the Viennese musicologist Erwin Ratz. Beethoven worked on the c♯ minor quartet op. 131 from the end of 1825 until August 1826. It was published

44 Ivan Mahaim, *Naissance et renaissance des derniers quatuors* (Paris, 1964), vol. 2.

45 Commentary thereupon to be found in the very knowledgeable selection on the late quartets in Paul Bekker, *Beethoven* (Berlin, n.d.), 516ff.

— posthumously — in June 1827 by Schott in Mainz with a dedication to Baron Joseph von Stutterheim and was first performed on June 5, 1828 in Halberstadt by the then famous touring string quartet of the Müller brothers. The last work of the group, the F major quartet op. 135, was composed between July and October 1826 and dedicated to the friend Johann Nepomuk Wolfmayer. Schlesinger of Paris published it in September of 1827 and it received its first performance on March 23, 1828 in Paris by the Schuppanzigh quartet. The replacement finale to op. 130, the last complete work by Beethoven, was written in autumn 1826 and published in May 1827 by Artaria. The first performance of the simultaneously but separately published fugue op. 133 was on January 20, 1853 in Paris.

The literature on the late quartets today is almost unsurveyably vast; almost throughout there are found descriptions of the stylistic peculiarities that separate these five quartets from Beethoven's earlier ones, as well as from those of his contemporaries: the immensely developed richness of detail work in voice leading, the attention to individual voices, the emphasis on formal counterpoint — which, already in the Handelian overture op. 124, was remarkably hard on the hearer — the new importance of the harmonic realm (especially the use of the church modes), the radicalization of the contrast within and among the movements and, finally, the use of conventionality, which in the middle quartets and particularly in the laconic style of the f minor quartet op. 95 yielded to sweeping individualization and thematic work. Thomas Mann had, together with Adorno, characterized this kind of conventionality in his *Doktor Faust.* "The relationship of late Beethoven to the conventional is for all its uniqueness and monstrousness of the formal language quite another thing, much more indulgent and kindly. Untouched, unchanged by the subjective, convention in the late works often appears barren, or, one might say, drained, self-forsaken, now a horrible and majestic personal venture."[46]

On this subject, Joseph Kerman has pointed to the inclusion of vocal forms, of musical lyric:[47] in the late quartets one finds recitative and aria, song, hymn, chorale and folk dance, an attempt to bring each vocal and mankind-uniting element (which in the ninth symphony could be shouted abroad) into the intimate chamber music genre through formal and gestural citation, to make it immanently present. For, as opposed to the f minor quartet, the late works largely lack all privately introspective tendencies, and this is how the quartets, despite their technically very abstract point of view, strike the listener outwardly; whoever apostrphizes them with analogy to the *Kunst der Fuge* — as *'Lesemusik'* — completely mistakes their intention and their actual form in sound.

Analogously to the three op. 59 quartets, these five quartets form (in quite an enlarged version) an internal unity: two quartets (op. 127 and op. 135, conventional in their four movements) frame three quartets which in stepwise fashion (from five movements in op. 132 to six movements with fugal finale in op. 130 to the interlinked seven movements of op. 131) distance themselves from formal conventions. Tonal connections embrace the single quartets, and the three middle works above all are — though it remains to be proven — thematically interrelated.

46 Thomas Mann, Doktor Faustus. *Das Leben des deutschen Tonsetzers Adrian Leverkühn erzählt von einem Freunde* (Frankfurt, 1967), 55.

47 Kerman, *loc. cit.*, 195ff.

The E♭ major quartet op. 127, in the traditional four movements, begins with a slow introduction reduced to the motto, a six measure *Maestoso* that takes on both punctuation and contrast functions. The main movement itself is expressly lyrical throughout and reminds one a bit of the first movement of the op. 101 piano sonata. The motto[48] opens not only the clearly formed 'four-square' exposition but the development as well, in which it appears in abbreviated form. The entrance of the recapitulation — otherwise relatively exact — is definitely obscured (measure proportions 74:91:73:43). The fundamentally lyrical character of the movement is expanded a bit to the 'marchlike' side solely with a folky neighbor idea accompanied in a decidedly 'primitive' fashion (m. 22ff.). The secondary theme, in the mediant key of g minor, continues the *cantabile* tone of the main theme, and is reminiscent of the developmental technique of the other E♭ major quartet op. 74, with flowing harmonies and canonic animation (m. 98–114). Using an inversion of the main theme, the coda continues the development work which here — as is usual in the late works — is much more motivic/combinatoric and freely variative than thematic or reductive. While the theme remains largely unaltered — as it already did at the beginning — the contrapuntal animation and variation of the middle and lower voices reminds one of the quartet style of later Haydn.

The slow movement, *Adagio, ma non troppo e molto cantabile* in A♭ major, likewise emphasizes the vocally melodic character of the themes; Kerman has pointed out reminders of the *Benedictus* of the *Missa solemnis* and the Leonore aria *"Komm, Hoffnung"* from *Fidelio*,[49] and,

48 Kerman, *loc. cit.*, 204ff.

49 Kerman, *loc. cit.*, 210.

technically as well as timbrally, one can also hear something of the *Adagio* of the ninth symphony. Beethoven here writes probably the most complex of his slow quartet movements, an amalgam of variation and three part form. A twenty measure theme (wide ranging and scarcely apt for conventional alterations) and six variations are so ordered harmonically and timbrally that the theme and variations 1 and 2 belong together, as do variations 4 through 6, while variation 3 in E major, a hymn comparable to that in the e minor quartet op. 59 no. 2, makes up the middle part. To be sure, E major is achieved without rulebook modulation, through the enharmonic reinterpretation of D^b major/$C\sharp$ major. Variation forms in slow movements are an important group within the late works, as in the ninth symphony op. 125, the piano sonata op. 111, and in the quartets op. 132 and 135; the stylistic and technical complexity − despite the immediate clarity of the form − is nevertheless brought to an otherwise unattained height in the E^b major quartet.

The dance movement, *Scherzando vivace,* in E major with an e^b minor trio is − in size and placement within this lyric quartet − a complete contrast to the first two, and to the last movement. Also found here are clear reminders of the scherzo of the ninth symphony. The movement opens with a pizzicato cadence that playfully harks back to the three tone cadence of the slow movement. But there follows a fugue opening, this time not related to op. 74, but rather to op. 95. Polyphonic and homophonic methods of elaboration alternate at close range until − the high point of the scherzos − two recitative-like insertions in 2/4 meter, with the two lower strings in unison, disturb this compact course. The trio, opening in e^b minor and quickly modulating through D^b major, b^b minor, D^b major, e^b minor and B^b major anticipates the *'Elfenton'* often apostrophized in Mendelssohn. Beethoven here begins to give up the five movement layout of the scherzo preferred in the middle quartets in that, after a complete scherzo recall, eleven trio measures appear as a reminiscence, as at the beginning of the finale of the ninth symphony. They are abruptly broken off and the movement closes with eight laconic measures of coda. The finale, in which Beethoven gives no tempo marking, rounds the quartet into a cycle with its links to the first movement. After a four measure chromatic prelude on the dominant, the movement opens its round dance of themes: reaching back once again to the 'foursquare' simplicity of the first movement the composer here rows up four folky, dancelike themes one after another.

Example 22

D

There follows one of the most comprehensive 'false recapitulations' in all of classical instrumental music (m. 97–144), into which Beethoven nevertheless builds combinatorial surprises. "He amuses himself by making frivolous combinations of the first theme and the third (m. 121ff.), by running away with the eighth note figure of the first theme."[50] Then follows the real recapitulation (m. 187ff.) which runs more or less exactly. Surprisingly, the movement closes with a C major coda in 6/8 meter, and although it is suggested, no new thematic material is introduced. The previously exposed themes are rhythmically re-formed and presented in inversion, and associations to the first movement and to the sixth variation of the slow movement (m. 109ff.) are also iserted. The teasing melodic play between A♭ and A that the composer carried on from the beginning of the finale (compare measures 5, 6 and 7), is finally decided in favor of A; the tritone is retained as an irritating element. The thematic material and the uneven phrase structure point to Haydnesque models, but the elaboration is quite otherwise: Beethoven's humor is stronger and more robust than that of the rather more polite Haydn.

The a minor quartet op. 132, which begins the closely interconnected 'middle' triad of late quartets, is in many ways the opposite of the E♭ major quartet. Not only has

50 Kerman, *loc. cit.*, 236.

Beethoven here, with five movements, given up the traditional formal scheme, but the concentration on a four note motive exposed at the beginning (the constructive and expressive center of the entire quartet) reinforces this dissolution of traditional formal categories. While in the E^b major quartet the lyrical element dominates, the principle of thematic contrast here penetrates the structure of the individual movements and thus undermines the principle of sonata form. The first movement, *Assai sostenuto . . . Allegro*, in a minor begins with an eight measure ṣlow introduction that exposes the four note motive (g♯ - a - f - e) and, as a fugue theme, also answers at the fifth and in inversion. The marchlike main theme of the movement is characterized by the four note motive, which can also be found in the scherzo and in the finale, and functions motivically in the fugue theme of the B^b major quartet op. 130 and the c^b minor quartet op. 131. The first movement of the a minor quartet uses the four note motive like a 'cantus firmus' (cf. m. 85ff., 103ff., 193ff.); the main theme of the movement behaves like a countersubject and thus remains remarkably 'figurative.' The exposition (m. 9—74) is distinct and clearly bounded and the modulating opening of the development appears relatively conventional. Nevertheless, after an abrupt general pause (m. 92) it is negated by new material that is at once developed canonically. Developmental work in the sense of motivic *'Fortspinnung'* and reduction is out of place there, where the synthetic character of the thematic material of the beginning is apparent. In place of an extended development, there appears a double reprise in e minor (m. 119—192) and a minor (m. 193—253) concluding with a coda (m. 254—264) that is as operatic and therefore 'figurative' as the second theme of the movement, which, with its trivial anticipatory accompaniment, rather reminds one of a Rossini cavatina. Two 'dance movements' surround the central slow movement of the a minor quartet, one an A major *Allegro ma non tanto*, a comprehensive study in double counterpoint based on a two measure motivic cell, the component parts of which are combined with each other and varied in such multifarious ways that only a measure by measure analysis can ring it to light. The model here — as in the minuet of op. 18 no. 5 — is the minuet from Mozart's string quartet KV 464; here also are found a four measure opening followed by voice combination in double counterpoint. A less thematically than rhythmically intricate trio, based on a melody from Beethoven's *Deutschen mit Coda* of 1790, forms the middle section of this movement.

Example 23

The second dance movement is the brief *Alla Marcia* in the three parts of a traditional minuet, and suggesting 3/4 meter in the upbeat construction of the theme at the beginning, making the half rest in the second measure seem too long. In its emphasis on dotted rhythm, this brief little movement is reminiscent of the *Scherzando* from the E^b major quartet op. 127.

Contrasting with the surrounding movements and having its own internal contrasts is the slow movement, the *Heiliger Dankgesang eines Genesenen an die Gottheit, in der lydischen Tonart*. Beethoven's involvement with church modes around 1820 must have been analogous to neo-classicism around 1920. It already appears in the *"Incarnatus"* of the *Missa solemnis,* and in the section *"Brüder, überm Sternenzelt"* in the choral finale of the ninth symphony. But it is hardly retrospective — even if Joseph Kerman may see it as perhaps an anticipation of the Palestrina revival of the nineteenth century[51] — but rather it appears to be a dialectic revolution, archaism as a step forward, reaching back as reaching ahead.

The five part chorale, in strict note against note texture, with the beginning of each chorale line led in by four voice head motive imitation, is twice interrupted by the D major section that Beethoven marked *Neue Kraft fühlend.* There are no connections or bridges between these sections and they are different in almost every respect: stepwise progression against disjunct melody, an almost mystical key lability against simple cadential harmony, chorale texture against virtuoso *obligato* counterpoint, a sense of timeless peace against active movement. Also missing are all mediating elements, yet the chorale does not appear uninfluenced by the D major episode. In its second appearance it is melodically ornamented (the movement's scheme can be described by the formula A B A′ B′ A″) and by its third appearance it is reduced to the canonically developed first chorale line and finally to the two tone motive f - e. Successive and variation forms thus are intertwined, and in particular the reshaping of the peculiarly archaic chorale into a highly complex contrapuntal study makes this quite distinct from a simple style citation.

The finale, *Piu Allegro . . . Allegro appassionato* in a minor, is introduced after the bagatelle-like *Alla Marcia* by an instrumental recitative, the beginning of which (in inversion) is related to the *"O Freunde, nicht diese Töne."*

51 Kerman, *loc. cit.,* 254.

In its triple course, its virtuoso three octave range (whose main tones anticipate the four tone motive, which then emerges in a 'crossed' form of f - g♯ - a - e), Beethoven creates a double contrast in sound — to the *Heiligen Dankgesang* as well as the *Alla Marcia*. The final movement itself is a sonata-rondo with an expanded coda; a vocal gesture connects the main theme of the first movement (also found here is the conventional operatic type of anticipatory accompaniment). The dancelike gestures, phrase structure and texture of the coda are related to the trio of the second movement. The connections in the coda serve not only to bring cyclic rounding to a rather dissociated work, but also cause the technical problems of the first movement to be dealt with again, among them an almost directly cited inclusion of contrapuntal elements (m. 244ff.), which are intentionally resolved in the course of a 'light' final close, analogous to the finale of op. 127, and in very sharp contrast to the final resolution of the following quartet, the *Grosse Fuge.*

If the succession of movements, the layout of the dance movement, the central position of the slow movement and the 'light' final resolution all show parallels between op. 127 and op. 132, such parallels exist (considering the original version of op. 130) between the two chronologically subsequent works, the op. 130 quartet in B♭ major and op. 131 in c♯ minor. The correspondences lie in the 'popular' genre dance movements (in the preceding group of works these were 'burdened' by counterpoint), in the unburdening of the slow movements — because there are two they are of course no longer in the central position — and in the climactic approach to the finale. Therefore, the meaning of the later composed lightweight finale of op. 130 is unclear in its proportions and in its thematic, motivic and harmonic goals.

The B♭ major quartet, that "monster of quartet music" as Schindler put it, begins with a sonata movement preceded by a slow introduction. Here the connections between *adagio* and *allegro* sections reach for new frontiers; the apparently clear scheme of the main movement's sonata form has been undermined and basic musical principles such as continuity and connection brought into question. Beethoven's struggle against convention is here manifest in two ways — in the violation of norms as well as in their overfulfillment, in both cases leaving the impression of something distorted, or destroyed. The slow introduction, traditional in its two part layout (the *Allegro* section breaks off after just five measures, endangering its conventionally structured gestural content) gains even more importance, and grows increasingly in the role of main theme. The regular secondary theme, reminiscent in its key of D♭ major of Schubertian modulation schemes, is a caricature of a lyric theme, derived motivically from the sixteenth figure and the chromaticism of the slow introduction. It has become permanently linked with the gesture of the "as if", and the G♭ major episode of the exposition (m. 72–88) seems like a citation from another piece (a Romantic piano piece in the style of the late Schubert Impromptus), as does the brief development (m. 95–132), which — after a short confrontation of *Adagio* and *Allegro* sections (here not really thematic, but rather gestural) — can indeed be traced motivically to the half step 'sigh' from the introduction and the sixteenth figure of the *Allegro,* though they certainly function as insertions. Not only continuity but, even more, unity of 'tone' are forsaken. Adorno's characterization of the late works is especially pertinent to this movement" "The force of the subjectivity (. . .) is the passionate gesture with which the art work abandons itself. It releases it, not in order to express itself, but rather in order inexpressively to shed the appearance of the art. It leaves behind mere ruins, and communicates, as with ciphers, only with the emptiness from which it has broken free."[52] "The caesuras, however (the precipitate breaking off that more than anything else characterizes the last works of Beethoven), are the impulses of this breaking out; the work is silent when it leaves off, and turns its cavity outwards."[53]

The three following movements fulfill the formal law, on the other hand, in what now seems like an 'equivocal' or 'suspicious' perfection; for example, in the scurrying *presto* with its drastic simplicity of form, its genuinely 'foursquare' course of melodic phrasing, and its simple juxtaposition of b$^\flat$ minor and B$^\flat$ major in scherzo and trio. Only the retransition to the scherzo (m. 48ff.) with its triple beginning on the diminished fourth c/e$^\flat$ /f$^\sharp$, its almost conversational question-answer play between first violin and *tutti*, breaks away from the predictable, reminding one — in particular in its gestural impulse — of those 2/4 measures in the scherzo of op. 127 that 'jump in' and of that almost irrational trespass into convention as it is found all over in the late works. The *andante con moto ma non troppo* with the noteworthy supplemental marking *poco scherzoso* is reminiscent in texture, independence of parts and tonal character of the D major *andante/Neue Kraft fühlend* from the a minor quartet op. 132; it lays no claim to the heaviness of a traditional slow movement, but rather remains graceful and lyrical, executed in rather clear sonata form — with such a virtuoso dominance of form that the irritations of the first move-

52 Adorno, *loc. cit.*, (see note 43), 16.

53 Adorno, *loc. cit.*, 17.

ment could not penetrate its almost hermetic beauty. The two first measures, indicated in the sketches as *'preludio,'* merit special mention. In them, Beethoven achieves a double contrast within the movement: in trasition from b♭ minor of the scherzo to D♭ major of the *Andante* (D♭ major, the key of the secondary theme in the first movement, is not parodistic here, but instead resolves the "as if"), and in the renewed use of the half step b♭ - a that had already opened the first movement.

Example 24

Finally, the *Alla Danza tedesca,* originally provided for op. 132 but then transposed to G major, likewise fulfills the traditional dance movement scheme with a trio, a varied *da capo* — apart from the figurative variations in the first violin (m. 90ff.) with its typical *'Bierfiedler-Figuren'* — and a brief coda in which, through the charming and almost serial interchange of theme measures (m. 130ff.), the soundscape of convention is again forever (figuratively) destroyed. Parallels can be drawn between the two dance movements of this quartet and those small, late piano pieces (after the piano sonatas) that Beethoven had published in two collections entitled *"Bagatellen"*, op. 119 and op. 126. Op. 126 no. 2 in g minor can be seen as a model for the b♭ minor scherzo, while the Bagatelle in D major op. 119 no. 3 in its *"à l'Allemande"* dance character points to the gesture and formal structure of the G major quartet movement.

The fifth movement of the B♭ major quartet bears the marking "Cavatina," another sign of the inclusion of vocal forms in instrumental music. As opposed to the opera aria, the cavatina is generally a shorter, rather songlike piece[54] usually serene in character, completely achieved here (with the first violin taking over the voice part). The range and shape of the vocal line, the accompaniment function of the other three parts, the rhetorical middle section with the C♭ major area that Beethoven marked *"beklemmt"* (oppressed) (m. 42–48), are all clear indications of the character of an "unwritten opera aria."[55] In the formal layout there are very clear correspondences with the Florestan aria from Beethoven's *Fidelio*[56] and the *"beklemmt"* section has a parallel in the *Arioso dolente* of the A♭ major piano sonata op. 110 where there is found the performance indication *"ermattet, Klagend"* (weary, lamenting). The ending is open, with that vocal gesture Beethoven favored in song conclusions, as in *"An die Hoffnung"* and *"Adelaide."* Though he did so in the symphony,

54 Cp. here the three cavatinas in Mozart's *Marriage of* Figaro, and Agatha's cavatina in Weber's *Freischütz*.

55 Kerman, *loc. cit.*, 199.

56 Kerman, *loc. cit.*, 196, for a very thorough analysis of the cavatina.

Beethoven shied away from using the voice in the string quartet (as Schönberg finally did). The cavatina, as imaginary aria, stops at the self-imposed boundaries of instrumental music.

The *Grand Fugue, tantot libre, tantot recherchée* forms the close of this quartet in three ways (a close that explains the subsequently composed finale as something of a softening to suite-like pleasantry). First, it corresponds (739 measures) to approximately the entire length of the preceding five movements, and thus creates that large scale two part form found again clearly in Mahler's symphonies. In the second place it resolves the formal crisis of the sonata movement left open in the first movement by means of an interpenetration of sonata form and fugue. Finally, it gathers in itself the characters of all three previous movements: the sonata — strong and laconic, the lyric-*cantabile*, and the scurrying scherzo type.[57]

The introduction, marked *ouvertura* (after the manner of an opera aria) presents the fugue theme, which (as has already been indicated) is derived from the slow introduction of op. 132. The presentation is a threefold harmonic statement, a rhythmic formation (and anticipation of the *allegro con brio* section) and an unfolding melody with harmonic support. The course of the fugue has many correspondences with a free sonata form, seeing (after the slow introduction) the B♭ major section (m. 25—157) and the G♭ major double fugue (m. 158—231) as an exposition, the *allegro con brio* section with the combination of thematic material (m. 232—530) as a development, the second

57 Cp. Kerman, *loc. cit.*, 268—302, and Hermann Scherchen, "Beethovens Grosse Fuge op. 133" in *Die Musik* 20 (1927—1928), 401—420, reprinted in Gerhard Schuhmacher (ed.), *Zur musikalischen Analyse* (Darmstadt, 1974), 161—185, and Warren Kirkendale, "The 'Great Fugue' op. 133. Beethoven's 'Art of Fugue' in *Acta Musicologica* 35 (1963).

Allegro con brio section (m. 531–654) as a finale, and the closing section with the intercalated citation of both double fugue themes (comparable throughout to the citation of the movement themes in the finale of the ninth symphony) as a coda (m. 661–739). Space prohibits a comprehensive analysis here, and reference to the cited secondary literature must suffice.

Example 25

In the B♭ major finale composed later, Beethoven takes up the *'Volkston'* of the fourth movement. In an anticipation of op. 135, where this happens to excess (though this 'anticipation' is chronologically a *'Nachgriff'*; the B♭ major finale was written after the completion of op. 135 in the winter of 1826) there follows that Haydn-esque sort of lightweight sonata-rondo, in definite disproportion to the size of the movement (494 measures), and — despite compositional fantasy in detail — is, in its unbroken texture, not free of classical traits.[58]

A fugue forms the close of the B♭ major quartet op. 130, and one forms the beginning of the c♯ minor quartet op. 131, that seven part quartet divided into a superorganized four movements that are probably the most thoroughly integrated of all the quartets. This integration is made clear in that the tempo sequence in the middle movement, variation section no. 4, truly reflects the tempo sequence of the large seven part form, making it a kind of seed or germ cell. And the unity goes farther: in rhythmic continuity, the thematic connection of opening fugue and finale, and in harmonic ordering, whereby the seven movements make up an expanded cadence without subdominant, but with a Neapolitan second step:

No. 1	No. 2	No. 3	No. 4	No. 5	No. 6	No. 7
c♯ minor	D major	b minor	A major	E major	g♯ minor	c♯ minor
I	II_n	VII	VI	III	V	I

In self ironic humor Beethoven wrote on the autograph: *"Nb. zusammengestohlen aus Verschiedenem, diesem und jenem."* (N.B. put together from various things, this and that.") which apparently upset the publisher Schott, for in a letter of August 19, 1826, the composer explained: "You wrote that it should be an original quartet; that stung me, so as a joke I wrote that it was put together. It is nonetheless brand new." In his Beethoven essay of 1870, Richard Wagner described the first movement, the c♯ minor *adagio* fugue thus: "The introductory, rather long *Adagio*, proba-

58 Kerman, *loc. cit.*, 367—374.

bly the most melancholy that has ever been expressed in sound, I might compare with arising in the morning of the day 'which in its long course shall not fulfill one wish, not one' (Faust). Yet at the same time it is a penance offering, a taking counsel with God out of belief in the eternal good."[59] Less poetically informed natures[60] stress in its analysis instead the perfection of the formal structure, the clarity of the divisions, the many layers of harmonic elements. The chromaticism inherent in the fugue theme operates strongly in the counterpoint and especially re-markable is the neat (in the traditional school fugue sense) fugal course in three values (whole notes, half notes and quarter notes) and, in the middle section (m. 67ff.), the two voice canon of upper and lower voices (m. 72ff.), the figurative dissolution of the melodic line of the fugue theme in new counterpoint (m. 91ff.), and the stretto and inversion sections. Different from the *Grosse Fuge*, which does not lack for interpenetration of contrapuntal and sonata movement principles, the opening fugue of the c♯ minor quartet is self-contained. Contrast is first found in the connection to the immediately following second movement, *Allegro molto vivace,* where in an almost monorhythmic, *perpetuum mobile* course are mixed the characteristics of a scherzo and the melodic leading of a rondo. Formally, however, it can be described as a sonata movement without development. The insufficiency of sonata form, already exhibited in op. 127, 132 and 130, here leads to an expansion of the harmonic and motivic distance among the individual movements.[61] "And now

59 Richard Wagner, *Sämtliche Schriften. Volksausgabe* (Leipzig, n.d.), vol. 9, 96.

60 Kerman, *loc. cit.,* 330ff.

61 Kerman, *loc. cit.,* 333.

(with the short transitional *Allegro moderato*) it is as if the master, secure in his skill, sets himself to his magic work; he now uses (*Andante*) the renewed strength of his own unique magic to fix in sound one of the most graceful forms, so that with it, happiest product of the deepest innocence, he may enchant himself restlessly in continually unheard variations, and through the radiant dawning of the eternal light, which breaks forth at his command."[62] The transitory *Allegro moderato*, little more than a free cadenza with inserted *Adagio,* forms the bridge to the central variation movement, *Andante ma non troppo e molto cantabile* in A major. The theme, with its persistent turn figure distributed between both upper voices, is the source for six variations, six individual 'bagatelles,' each distinct in character. The first variation is largely figurative, but at the same time exposes a double dotted motive that makes another appearance in the first movement of the F major quartet op. 135. The second, *Piu mosso,* strikes a hearty dance tone. In the third, *Andante moderato e lusinghiero,* are found two correspondences: the first is technical, relating to the canon section of the first movement; the other, motivic, to the main theme of the first movement of the a minor quartet op. 132:

Example 26

op. 132
I, 11

op. 131
IV, 98

62 Wagner, *loc. cit.,* 97.

In an analysis, Donald Tovey[63] has also referred to parallels with the *"Benedictus"* canon in the *Missa solemnis*. The fourth variation, *Adagio*, presents the theme in double counterpoint and inversion, while the fifth, *Allegretto*, does without polyphonic or technical artifice, and hones the theme down to its harmonic skeleton by means of motivic reduction. *'Bordun'* effects, which already played a role in the trio of op. 132, are also used. The sixth variation, *Adagio ma non troppo e semplice*, shows that specific type of 'note against note' hymn texture, dramatized solely through the sixteenth figure in the cello (m. 195ff.) that 'leaps in' at the beginning. This figure is nevertheless then integrated into the melodic structure and harmonically intensified (m. 211ff.), and, finally, prepares the concertant half-variation (m. 220–230) which, cadenza-like, leads to the enlarged theme (in the sense of a scherzo in C major and F major with a 'trio' in a major and a rather brief coda).

The seven part structure that had dominated in the fourth section of the quartet also plays a role in the following *Presto* in E major (n. 5). Once again Beethoven shuns a simple declaration of the *'ton'*: elements are found in the variation movement of the slow and of the scherzo type. Similarly, characteristics of the scherzo are here combined with melodic elements of a rondo movement. Already in the op. 59 quartets, Beethoven had enlarged the traditional three part structure of scherzo-trio-scherzo to a five part form. Here he now proceeds — through a triple (though indeed altered) trio recall — to a seven part structure. The unity of the movement is confirmed by tonal exclusivity (E major remains the fundamental

63 Donald Francis Tovey, "Some aspects of Beethoven's art forms" in Tovey, *Essays and Lectures on Music* (London, 1949).

tonality for all scherzo and trio sections, while A major, as the key of the foregoing, and g♯ minor as key of the following movement play only a small role), as well as through the clear relationship of the scherzo theme and the three trio themes:

Example 27

The *Adagio quasi un poco Andante* in g minor (no. 6) has a function analogous to that of the *Allegro moderato* (no. 3): transition, harmonic articulation (the dominant function with regard to the following finale) and separation, with otherwise the same character. Above all it carries, in clearly comprehensible form (two measure introduction — a a b a b a — two measure sequencing cadence) reminders of the cavatina of the B$^\flat$ major quartet op. 130, or at least of its simple vocal tone. And then the finale: "This is the dance of the world itself: wild joy, painful lamentation, love's enchantment, highest desire, moaning, rage, lust and suffering. There it quivers like lightning, the storm roars, and standing over all the colossal music-maker who compels and forbids, stepping strong and sure from whirlwind to whirlpool, leading to the abyss. Then he smiles to himself, for to him this magic has only been a game."[64] This finale, *Allegro* in c$^\sharp$ minor, is in almost every respect the crowning glory of the quartet: in expressivity as well as in intensity, in thematic-motivic integration as well as in harmonic plan and in the unquestioned mastery of sonata form — until now held in reserve. The final problem, solved in op. 130 only in the form of an oversized fugue that strained at the bounds of the genre, is here given a "most nearly perfect solution,"[65] and indeed within a sonata form whose 'normality' is surprising. Thematic contrast, modulatory areas, an extended and intensive development, an expansive and triumphal recapitulation (as hadn't been found in the quartets since op. 59 no. 2) and a summarizing coda — all these coexist without a rupture, without a montage of foreign elements, but in a concentration and terseness

64 Wagner, *loc. cit.*, 97.

65 Kerman, *loc. cit.*, 341.

reminiscent of op. 95 (which, particularly, does without thematic transitions). A two part main theme constructed of anapestic and iambic rhythm, with a unison head motive that also functions as connective and bridge material; a secondary theme whose shape is taken directly from the fugue theme, producing the cyclic rounding of the quartet; and finally a recall in the development of the modulation plan of the fugue, are all presented in a clearly balanced layout (measure proportions 77:82:104. 135). Here Beethoven summarizes all those questions, problems and possible solutions that had arisen since the E♭ major quartet op. 127.

The F major quartet op. 135, the composer's last completed work, draws a summary in another way: the size of the demands are definitely reduced in an almost classicizing homage to both great models Haydn and Mozart, thereby making a connection to the op. 18 no. 2 and op. 18 no. 5 quartets, and the symphony in F major op. 93, with more parallels than just tonality. The F major *allegretto* is a Haydnesque sonata movement in a balanced, symmetrical form as was last found in the e minor quartet op. 59 no. 2. It has internal contrast, contrasting theme structure, an extended transition which, after the manner of Mozart,[66] is in the dominant (though based on the tonic) area, and a Haydnesque 'false recapitulation' within its two part development (m. 81ff.). The coda (m. 186ff.) exhibits a classical key relationship and classical formal proportions (measure relationships 57:43:58:35). The F major scherzo, reminiscent of analogous forms in op. 74 and op. 127, does not take such a retrospective viewpoint, but rather has a 'will o' the wisp' effervescence, in the almost sneaky entry of triple counterpoint, in syncopating cross rhythms

66 Kerman, *loc. cit.*, 357.

and an apocalyptic[67] trio/scherzo complex common in the late works; Thus it is found in the D♭ major *lento assai, cantante e tranquillo* which — in the smallest space and with renewed emphasis on the vocal element — once again challenges the variation principle, here in two ways: figuratively and in the sense of character variation, thereby depending throughout on specific expressive 'levels,' as in the cavatina. Lastly, the finale is superscribed with a statement that has generated many anecdotes:[68] "The hard sought answer: Must it be? It must be!" On a twelve measure slow introduction functioning as an opera scene parody there follows a sonata movement built symmetrically like the first movement, brief and comprehensible as well, with quotations from the slow introduction before the recapitulation and coda and with a humorously specific citation from the E major scherzo of the c♯ minor quartet (m. 44ff.). "The riddle-like motto and its biographical reference make the basic motivation of this work quite clear: it is the tendency to isolate convention on several levels at the same time — as convention of the

---

67 Kerman, *loc. cit.*, 360.

68 Here is often recounted the anecdote of the money hungry housewife, or that of the quartet dilletante Ignaz Dembscher who, having missed the subscription for the B♭ major quartet, wanted to borrow the parts from Beethoven himself. He only got them, however, on terms strictly cash. Through Adolf Bernhard Marx the additional information transpires: " . . . The author has received the following report from his dear friend, Moritz Schlesinger. In 1819 and the following years Herr Schlesinger was a member of his father's publishing company which had, among others, accepted the F major quartet for publication. Under date of February 27, 1859 he wrote to this author on the occasion of a new edition the following: " . . . as for the 'Es muss sein' in the last quartet, no one can clear it up for you better than I. For I possess that same work in his own hand, written out in parts, and when he sent it to me he wrote: "You can see what an unlucky man I am, not only has it become quite difficult to write — I was thinking of writing something much bigger, and only wrote this because I promised it to you and needed money — but with what difficulty it came to me you can decipher . . . from the *'Es muss sein.'* " (quoted from Adolph Bernhard Marx, *Beethoven* (Berlin, 1906), vol. 2, 450–451.

genre style created by Haydn and as convention of Beethoven's peculiar late style — and so to surmount it, in order that it shift suddenly in a quite new, personally impersonal language. The unique sparseness, indeed incomprehensibility of the expression, the refusal to make any retrospective reference to the three preceding quartets and the likewise definite but formally scaled down connection to op. 127 here have their deepest roots. They are, at the same time, a signal unmistakeable for anyone who 'has really studied' Beethoven's late quartets that with op. 135 an end has been made."[69]

69 Ludwig Finscher, notes accompanying the recording of the late quartets by the Vegh Quartet on Telefunken, SKA 25113—T/1—4, p. 4. (German release).

Franz Schubert

Schubert's string quartets — about twenty in all, according to Otto Erich Deutsch[1] (three presumed lost, four incomplete or only single movements) — were written btween 1812 and 1826, thus contemporary with the middle and late quartets of Beethoven. Schubert's time and place proximity to Beethoven is always stressed in the literature, especially concerning the evolution of comparable genres (symphonies, string quartets, piano sonatas). This emphasis is almost a *"leitmotiv"* and represents that viewpoint — often explicit and often without truly considering the situation, that sets Beethoven up as model, against which Schubert's divergences are compared and hence often censured. Without doubt Beethoven's music played an important role for the younger man, but this influence has surely been much exaggerated. In fact, should one endeavor — without depending on the literature — to analyze the works in question, Beethoven's influence on the composition of these quartets would appear to have been rather small.

Several fundamental points must be established here. For one thing, Schubert's early quartets, composed by the fifteen and sixteen year old school boy in 1812 and

---

1 Otto Erich Deutsch, *Schubert. Thematic Catalogue of all his works in chronological order* (London, 1951); also Deutsch, "The chronology of Schubert's string quartets" in *Music and Letters* 34 (1943), 25–30, and Deutsch (ed.), *Schubert. Die Dokumente seines Lebens* (Kassel, Bärenreiter, 1964).

1813, were intended for the family quartet at home and were therefore *Hausmusik* in the sense that is indebted to Haydn. For another thing, the earlier quartets were a medium in which the young composer practiced sonata form, unlike Beethoven who did this in his early piano works, and whose op. 18 quartets — works of a thirty year old — were neither *Hausmusik* in the sense of amateur performance, nor exercises in compositional technique. Borrowings from Beethoven found in these early quartets are not usually from chamber music, but rather from the first two symphonies. In Schubert's maturity, which began about 1817, there is, for example in the piano sonatas, a clear comparison to be made with the mighty model. But apart from the forsaken quartet project of the winter of 1820, of which there remains solely the c minor movement D. 703, the string quartet cannot be so compared, and in the three works of 1824 and 1826 (a minor D. 804, d minor D 810, G major D. 887) Schubert is such an independent, individual composer that Beethoven no longer plays any role as model, and indeed was hardly influential in the late works at all.

Eleven of Schubert's fifteen string quartets with at least a single movement were written between 1812 and 1816 (with the exception of the E major quartet op. 125 no. 2, D. 353) for the family quartet consisting of the brothers Ignaz and Ferdinand, their father, and Schubert himself, and they therefore served at the same time as practice material for the home ensemble and for the developing skills of the young composer, who wrote these works in part — as corrections on the autographs show — under the scrutiny of his composition teacher Antonio Salieri, or at least showed the works to him.

Up to the op. 125 pair of quartets published in 1830 by Czerny, all the earlier quartets of Schubert first appeared

in the late 1870's in single editions and then shortly before
the turn of the century in the complete edition prepared
by Eusebius Mandyczewski. By this time many autographs
were already scattered or lost. In our century various single
movements turned up again that could be ordered among
the early works, thanks in particular to the researches of
Maurice J. E. Brown.[2]
The chronology of the early works is known today with
relative certainty.[3] Schubert's fastidious writings on the
autographs (where these are preserved) leave hardly any
doubts, and the inexplicable dating of the E^b major quartet op. 125 no. 1 in the year 1824 (because of this it still
was ordered high — tenth — in the old complete edition,
but this has since been corrected), and the rediscovered
manuscript dated the work in November 1813.
Schubert's first surviving string quartet in "changing
keys," probably from the summer of 1812 (D. 18), has
evoked negative comment throughout the literature.[4]
There is indeed much that is unrhymed and imperfect,
but the basis of the criticism probably lies in a comparison
of the work with Beethoven. The model here, however, as
numerous contrapuntal and fugal elements in particular
show, was the more traditional fugue quartet of an Albrechtsberger or Monn, which indeed also provided a
model for Beethoven's early quartet fugues. In addition,
many technical elements — found only in the first work —
appear to have been borrowed from the quartets of

2 Maurice J. E. Brown, *Schubert. A critical biography* (London, 1958);
German translation: Wiesbaden, 1968.

3 Deutsch, "The chronology . . ."

4 See for example Alfred Einstein, *Schubert. Ein musikalisches Porträt*
(Zürich, 1952), 42ff.; Gerald Abraham, *The music of Schubert* (New
York, Norton, 1947), 88ff.; Hans-Martin Sachse, "Franz Schuberts Streich-
quartette," (diss., Münster, 1958), 43ff.

Haydn: monothematicism in the sonata movements, irregularity of phrase and period structure in the slow and final movements, dance character of the minuet which is always the third movement (only the above-mentioned E^b major quartet op. 125 no. 1, D. 87, has a scherzo, which — apparently through a change made by the publisher — stands in second place). Moreover, Schubert's layout of the slow movements in particular appears to have been influenced by the middle quartets of the Viennese period, since the "Serenaden-Quartette op. 3 nr. 5" (published by Roman Hofstetter under Haydn's name) appears to have stood godfather to the F$^\sharp$ major *andante* of the first quartet.

Between the summer of 1812 and the winter of 1813, thus within a scant year and a half, Schubert wrote (each within a few days or weeks at most) six more string quartets: no. 2 in C major D. 32, completed on September 30, 1812; no. 3 in B^b major D. 36, between November 19, 1812 and February 21, 1813; no. 4 in C major D. 46, from the third to the seventh of March 1813; no. 5 in B^b major D. 68 (only two movements survive), between June 8 and August 18, 1813; no. 6 in D major D. 74, which Schubert dedicated to his father for his name day, finished on September 22, 1813; and no. 10 in E^b major op. 125 no. 1, D. 87 in November 1813. In all these works the influence of Haydn and Mozart is constantly perceptible. But beginning with the second quartet, Schubert's personal style begins to evolve — in detail, in the security of compositional technique, and in the fundamentally unique concept of the function of first movement sonata form. This is expressed for example in the moderation of the movement tempos and the renunciation of *adagio* forms in particular. Schubert's slow movements in these early quartets are consistently songlike or in a serenade style. The first movements, with far more of a finale than an opening feeling in the quartets no. 2 and 3, strive toward sonata form, not in the sense of Beethoven's motivic elaboration, but rather — again with a basis in Haydn's middle quartets, in particular op. 50 — with monothematic development of individual themes based on common melodic and rhythmic material, but distinguished by their apparent form and particularly by the nature of the accompaniment. The accompaniment, though still often relatively schematic, already has that dominating function, which in the mature works no longer allows one merely to consider the theme in isolation. Along with this shift of compositional priorities comes an emphasis on harmony: specifically, Schubert used the development sections more for the harmonic coloration of his material than for development and alteration of the motives and themes. Finally, the composer facilitated large scale formal articulation of the sonata movement by basing entire sections on a common rhythmic pattern, as in the first movement of the third quartet, the recapitulation of which runs in continuous triplets, while the exposition is based on an eighth note rhythm.

This third quartet, as a model for which Einstein correctly pointed to Haydn's d minor quartet op. 76 no. 2,[5] is particularly interesting with regard to its slow movement which begins with a six measure theme, hemiolic and songful. But the middle section creates a definite tone color contrast, leading to a dark (in range and timbre) c♭ minor area, from the beginning of which appear contrasting tremolo passages. These have often been considered (up to the G major quartet D. 887) orchestral effects in Schubert and really foreign to the quartet, ignoring the fact that

5 Einstein, *loc. cit.*, 42.

the composer here was not trying to achieve effects of intensification as in orchestral composition (tremolos are mostly confined to the piano works) but rather seeking both colorfully effective as well as rhythmically uncontoured timbral levels without motivic structural function. With these tremolos, and with rather large pizzicato sections (already found in Beethoven) there begins to be seen a structurally, timbrally and technically evolving quartet style, which may be considered a forerunner of the quartet style of the second half of the twentieth century.

Although relatively restricted in their development, Schubert's early quartets do always show experimental details, as in the almost Baroque middle section of the *Andante* in the highly chromatic C major quartet D. 44 (the minuet of which contains the above mentioned borrowings from the scherzo of Beethoven's first symphony op. 21). In the last movement of the quartet no. 5, D. 68, Schubert tries his hand at a Haydnesque final 'surprise' but without commanding the model's witty brevity.[6] The first scherzo in the E^b major quartet D. 87 with its *Ländler* trio, is likewise based on Haydn, while its finale, one of the most successful last movements in the early works, shows a command of proportion and rhythmic wit. The following four quartets (augmented by a fragmentary single movement in d minor D. 103, discovered in our century, completed and edited by Alfred Orel), were written between 1814 and 1816: the D major quartet no. 7, D. 94 in 1814; the B^b major quartet no. 8, supplied by the publisher with the confusingly high opus no. 168, D. 112, between September 5 and 13, 1814 (on the first page of the manuscript the seventeen-

---

6 On this subject, see Bernd Sponheuer, "Haydns Arbeit am Finalproblem" in *AfMw* 34 (1977), 199ff., esp. 222.

year-old composer proudly wrote: "completed in 4 1/2 hours"); the first minor quartet — apart from single movements — no. 9 in g minor, D. 173, between March 25 and April 1, 1815 and the quartet no. 11 in E major op. 125 no. 2, D. 353 (which for a long time was likewise dated 1824) in 1816. Two essential factors differentiate these four works from the earlier ones: a perfectly developed command of the traditional movement schemes and their fulfillment, leading — in particular in the g minor quartet — to an almost 'classicistic' regularity of the form at times, and besides this an increase in the technique, even virtuosity, demanded of the performers. Thus one assumes that quartets no. 9 and no. 11 were not likely to have been written for the home quartet with its limited resources. In the E major quartet one presumes[7] a performance for a private musical society in Vienna, probably by a professional ensemble. Moreover, the influences of classical quartet composition still have their effect, but are on the one hand so sublimated and on the other so obvious that one might at times almost believe that the composer is consciously reaffirming the tradition. This is especially true in the slow movement of the B major quartet D. 112, which in its overall form as well as in its use of the characterizing accompaniment figure is related to Mozart's quartet KV 465, and in the g minor quartet, with a minuet based on the g minor symphony KV 550, the finale of which is reminiscent of Haydn's quartet op. 20 no. 3 with its sound of a 'brightened' g minor. Some small evidences of a compositional crisis in the year 1817 (indicated for example by the numerous fragmentary piano sonatas[8]) are found in the E major

7 Deutsch, *Thematic catalogue.*

8 See Hans Koeltzsch, *Franz Schubert in seinen Klaviersonaten* (Leipzig, 1927).

quartet D. 353. Here the movements' proportions are distorted, and the conflict between rather terse motivic development and the harmonically variable expansion of thematic material (requiring much more musical space) remains undrawn. Static-timbral and dynamic-structural composition are immediately juxtaposed here, and the Beethovenian tradition — also with respect to the expansion to virtuoso concert quartet, to music for performance — gets distorted. "The other of the epoch-making works is the string quartet movement in c minor from December 1820 (D. 703). There are no bridges to it from the earlier quartets."[9] Alfred Einstein's statement characterizes the solitary place (comparable to the b minor symphony) of this incomplete quartet (an $A^\flat$ major *Andante* breaks off after 41 measures) which in the evolution of Schubert's personal style can only be understood in the light of the "fragmentary piano sonatas" from the years 1817 to 1819. Quite striking here is the free handling, rich in fantasy, of the sonata movement scheme which up to that point held the relatively unquestioned function of formal framework in the early quartets. Here the conflict presented in the E major quartet is clearly drawn and more rigorously than anywhere else in all the quartets and, as a result, the Schubert literature has many disagreements over the formal course of this dramatically intense movement. Einstein[10] and Walter Riezler[11] consider the rather more figurative than melodic beginning as the main theme — mainly on functional harmonic grounds. Hans-Martin Sachse[12] attempts an analysis that sees the

9 Einstein, *loc. cit.*, 187f.

10 Einstein, *loc. cit.*, 188.

11 Walter Riezler, *Schuberts Instrumentalmusik* (Zurich, 1967), 27f.

12 Sachse, *loc. cit.*, 215ff.

beginning — analogous to the bass line in the b minor symphony — as an introduction with the first theme entering in measure 27. This is in spite of the fact that within a c minor movement the first theme is thus in A^b major and that this first theme takes no part whatsoever in the events of the development, remaining episodic as in many Haydn movements. Yet his assumption does address the fact that the recapitulation, otherwise relatively complete, does without the beginning of the movement, which is brought back later as a *quasi* coda.

Example 28

There is, perhaps, a way out of this dilemma. It appears possible to me that classical compositional principles as based on the differentiation of theme characters apparently had only limited value for Schubert in these years. More important for thematic stabilization are distinctions and contrasts of a musical character — of compositional gesture —, and thus the dramatic-dynamic beginning enters into the main theme area, even though because of its figurative nature it hardly conforms to a melodic contour, and dominates, once again not in motivic development, but rather in timbre, in motion, in dynamics, and in the rhythmic ostinati within the development section. Here cyclic rounding might be sufficient reason for the presence of the section with its reminiscent recall. While the section that stands for the main theme hardly achieves thematic solidity, the lyric-*cantabile* part, that substitutes for the secondary theme is so definitely structured that — with its songlike form, self-enclosed and recurring in three analogous guises — it has a rather static-episodic effect and — in a continuation of Haydn's compositional principles — disavows developmental elements of the sonata principle, having instead something of the sound and structural quality of a slow movement. This fundamental redundancy may be the reason why Schubert broke off the second movement.

While for the early and middle string quartets there are no accounts in Schubert's own words or references in letters or critiques, the situation is different for the last three works, composed between 1824 and 1826. On March 31, 1824, Schubert wrote to his friend Leopold Kupelweiser: "I have created little that is new in my songs; on the contrary I sought to do this in several instrumental pieces. I have composed two quartets for violin, viola and violoncello and an octett, and still want to write a quartetto. In any case I want to pave the way to the great symphony in this manner."[13] The "two quartets" refer to the quartet no. 13 in a minor op. 29 no. 1, D. 804, and the quartet no. 14 in d minor, D. 810, while the planned third refers to the quartet in G major op. 161,

13 Quoted from Deutsch, *Dokumente*, 230.

D. 887, of which sketches have been found dating from 1824. All three quartets should have been published under the op. no. 29 but in Schubert's lifetime only the a minor quartet was published, in September 1824 by Sauer & Leidesdorf of Vienna. The a minor quartet, written in February 1824, is apparently the first to have been performed, on March, 14, 1824 in a concert by the Schuppanzigh quartet at the Vienna *"Musikverein"* in the 'red eagle' room. On the same day the painter Moritz von Schwind wrote in a letter to his and Schubert's mutual friend Schober about the work's impression: "Schubert's quartet was performed, rather slowly according to his intention, but very purely and tenderly. It is on the whole very gentle, but is of the kind that lets a melody linger, like a song, with great feeling and very well expressed. It got much applause, especially the minuet, which is extraordinarily tender and natural."[14]

Correspondent's reports on the quartet in the Vienna and Leipzig *Allgemeine Musikalische Zeitung*[15] yield almost no information, thus showing the small role Schubert played in the musical life of the Austrian capital.

Schubert quotes himself in the two middle movements of the quartet. The theme of the *Andante* comes from the music of the third entr'acte to Wilhelmine von Chézy's drama *Rosamund, Fürstin von Zypern* (D. 797, 1823) and the main motive of the minuet comes from the song *"Schöne welt, wo bist du"* on Schiller's poem *"Götter Griechenlands"* (D. 677, 1819).

14 Quoted from Deutsch, *Dokumente*, 230.

15 *Allgemeine Musikalische Zeitung*, Vienna, March 27, 1824: 'New quartet by Schubert. This composition should be listened to several times in order that one might pronounce a fundamental judgement on it." *Allgemeine Musikalische Zeitung*, Leipzig, April 29, 1824: "First quartet by Schubert: as a firstfruit not at all to be despised."

Unlike the c minor movement, Schubert fulfills the sonata movement scheme here in the first movement of the a minor quartet,[16] but only in order to, in his view, upset it that much more. The tonal relations do indeed correspond, but there is no distinction of characters between the main and secondary themes, both of which are lyric-contemplative. Instead, differences are found especially between thematic sections and transitional parts, which Schubert makes more important spatially and thematically. These no longer serve simply to bridge thematic parts, but function just as much as developmental and contrasting material. The wide ranging field, growing by means of its own variative processes, is contrasted by brief, motivically altered, dynamically delineated statements. The time-space continuum of the movement is not, as with Beethoven, one linear thread with different, distinct elements of the peaceful and the explosive that evolve in timbre at the same time. This 'reverse functioning' of the sonata movement principle, its penetration by static or self-inclusive cyclic elements (not limited to the late quartets), not only expresses Schubert's individuality, but also is the starting point for a development in the nineteenth and early twentieth centuries, which until today has been largely disregarded in favor of the Beethoven-Brahms-Schoenberg line.

The C major *Andante,* in two parts (A-A'), is less interesting in structure than in harmony. As in the G major quartet and the C major quintet op. 163, D. 956, the immediate adjacency of major and minor is an important structural element. A primarily mediant harmonic progression, half tone shifts and enharmonic reinterpre-

16 See the analytical remarks in Einstein, *loc. cit.,* 289ff.; Sachse, *loc. cit.,* 227ff.; Riezler, *loc. cit.,* 49ff.

tation are also found here.[17] The minuet, with its un-
disturbed balance between formal structure and tonal
character, belongs among the most perfect movements
of Schubert the lyricist, who achieves here — on an a
minor foundation — a smooth and static character of
sound by juxtaposing phrases in modal harmonizations
without leading tone. The finale, moderated in tempo
like the first movement though less densely structured,
harks back to the Haydnesque type of sonata-rondo
movement. It has no regular development and instead
introduces development elements into transitional sections, while the second theme, once again primarily
rhythmic, is merely episodic.

Still to be mentioned is the form of the accompaniment. In the first movement, as in the finale, Schubert
particularly distinguishes the metric aspect of the accompaniment, and he layers several rhythmic patterns of
different phrase lengths over one another — at its clearest
in the closing part of the last movement.

17 Cf. Elmar Seidel, "Die Enharmonik in den harmonischen Grossformen
Franz Schuberts" (diss. Frankfurt, 1962).

Example 29

M. 113

The d minor quartet no. 14, D. 810, which Schubert began immediately after completion of the a minor quartet, was not finished until January 1826. It was first performed on February 1, 1826 at the home of the *Hofkapell* singer Josef Barth by an *ad hoc* ensemble. The first public performance took place five years after Schubert's death, on March 12, 1833, in Berlin. The quartet was one of the first to be printed and was published posthumously in 1831, by Joseph Czerny in Vienna, who a year before had already brought out the op. 125 quartets. The composer Franz Lachner, who since 1822 belonged to Schubert's circle of friends, reported in his memoires on a further private performance at his home: "The . . . quartet, which at present enchants the whole world, and is .counted among the greatest creations of its genre, did not receive unqualified applause throughout. The first violinist Sch. (probably Ignaz Schuppanzigh) who, to be sure because of his advanced age, was not up to the task, said to the composer after the reading: 'Brother, there is really nothing good about this; stick to your songs,' whereupon Schubert silently packed up the parts and kept them ever afterward in his desk."[18] This is a somewhat romanticized account which may hardly be relied on, for it originated fifty years later, and Schuppanzigh was at the time of the story just fifty years old and technically still quite capable of Beethoven quartets. His negative judgement could have come about as a result of what he had just learned from Beethoven's works. Schubert also quotes himself in this quartet. As he had already done in the A major piano quintet op. 114, D. 667 (1819) and in the flute variations on *"Trockene Blumen"* in e minor op. 160, D. 802 (1824),

18 Otto Erich Deutsch, Schubert. *Die Erinnerungen seiner Freunde* (Leipzig, 1957), 249.

he bases the slow movement on an actual song, here his
setting of Mathias-Claudius' *"Der Tod und das Mädchen"*
(D. 531) from 1817.

The d minor quartet is Schubert's gloomiest and at the
same time most dramatic.[19] Its minor mode in all four
movements is only brightened at the close of the slow
movement and in the trio of the dance movement. With
respect to form it follows the lead of the a minor quartet
in fulfilling the sonata movement scheme, but with other
structural functions. Much as in the c minor movement,
the first movement begins with an introduction that is
hardly concise in thematic material (m. 1—40). This is
missing in the recapitulation, and is taken up again in part
only in the coda. As in the movement from 1820 the
very same rhythmic and melodic material of this beginning continues through the whole movement, indeed
it characterizes the whole quartet, in which — as is otherwise scarcely known in Schubert — there are evidences
of cyclic unification. While the main theme material
functions first of all as a rhythmic foundation, the relatively brief development primarily works with the thematic material of the secondary theme. Still more important
than this motivic elaboration are the harmonic re-colora-
tions in the recapitulation of the exposition and poly-
rhythmic layering, which superimposes theme sections
and various accompaniment elements upon one another:

19 See the analyses in Riezler, *loc. cit.*, 82ff.; Sachse, *loc. cit.*, 251ff.

Example 30

M. 102

An important structural element here, as well as in the C major symphony D. 944, is the opposition of triplet and dotted rhythm: 𝅘𝅥𝅮𝅘𝅥𝅮𝅘𝅥 vs. 𝅘𝅥𝅭𝅘𝅥𝅮 . The g minor *Andante,* one of the least chamber musical of variation movements, is regular in construction throughout. The 24 measure theme, through rearrangement, contraction and addition of a new middle part taken from the song, is figuratively altered in five variations that leave the length, structure, articulation and harmonic course untouched. In the first variation, the first violin line dissolves into triplets and contrapuntal figuration, and in the second, melodic variants of the theme in the upper register of the cello are combined with three different accompaniment figures. In a metric diminution of the main theme, the third variation is based on a continual rhythm, the fourth in G major breaks into triplets while the fifth combines the thematic form of the second variation with triplet, dotted and sixteenth note accompaniments, leading to the climax of rhythmic intensity, to a multi-level structure comparable to the first movement, out of which the coda emerges, becoming simpler and bringing back the theme.

The scherzo, quite short as compared with the other movements, is based on a syncopated theme, and creates — in combining the characters of the first and second movements — dynamic and timbral contrasts within a small space, in the scherzo itself as well as the D major trio, a gentle *Ländler,* almost sweet in its expression.

While the violin figurations of the fifth variation of the slow movement already pointed to Beethoven's op. 47 violin sonata in A major as a model, this impression is reinforced in the finale, a frenzied, wide-ranging d minor *presto* over 700 measures long. Formally a sonata-rondo with brief developmental elements and appended stretto, the movement has at the same time thematic reminiscences of the scherzo and first movement. Structurally important here are long stretches in unison that help to articulate the form, thus creating a strong, structured shape by means of sound. While the main theme keeps the same character, the secondary theme appears in three ways: with sharp attacks, counterpointed by a triplet chain in the cello, and in a lyrical reinterpretation. As already found in the a minor quartet, there are also rhythmic patternings, attempts at timbral structuring, and harmonic areas that establish the individuality of this work and its place with the quartets of Beethoven — though ultimately foreign to the latter's compositional principles.

Schubert's last string quartet, no. 15 in G major, op. 161 (D. 887), was written in the space of ten days in June 1826. From one of Schubert's letters,[20] it transpires that in March 1827 a private performance had apparently been given at the home of his friend Lachner. In February 1828 Schubert offered the piece for printing, together with the d minor quartet and numerous other works, to the publisher Schott in Mainz, but without success. The first movement of the quartet was performed on March 26, 1828 in a public concert arranged and directed by Schubert himself, by memebers of the Schuppanzigh quartet, with Joseph Böhm substituting for the ill first violinist. There are almost no reviews,[21] since Vienna was at that time under the influence of Paganini-mania. The first performance of the whole quartet took place on

20 Schubert to Lachner, letter of March 5, 1827: ' Be so good as to give the bearer of this message the score and written out parts of my quartet in G major, since Slawic promised me to come to you Wednesday evening." Quoted from Deutsch, *Dokumente, loc. cit.,* 413.

21 *Allgemeine Musikalische Zeitung,* Leipzig, May 7, 1828: ". . . 1. A new violin quartet; full of spirit and originality, performed by Messrs. Böhm, Holz, Weiss and Linke . . .". Quoted from Deutsch, *Dokumente, loc. cit.,* 504.

December 8, 1850 by the Hellmesberger quartet, which had premiered numerous Schubert quartets. The work was first printed in 1851 by Diabelli in Vienna.

The G major quartet,[22] which to this day lags behind the more popular quartets in a minor and d minor in both the performance tradition and in general appreciation, probably owes its less enthusiastic reception to its considerable length and technical demands on the performers, while on the other hand that openly obliging accessibility is missing, especially in the slow movement. Thus in formal, timbral and harmonic respect this is another step beyond the advances of the d minor quartet. Even the emblematic emphasis on an equivocal major/minor chord at the beginning of the first movement (found again in the string quintet in C major and at work in Gustav Mahler's sixth symphony) has, in its stress on timbral distinctions and on modal conflict, left an important evolutionary mark on the harmonic thinking of the nineteenth century.

Example 31

22 See the analyses in Riezler, loc. cit., 92ff.; Sachse, *loc. cit.*, 282ff.; Judy Gillett, "The problem of Schubert's G major string quartet D. 887" in *Music Review* 35 (1974), 281–291, and Carl Dahlhaus, 'Schuberts letztes Streichquartett" *Musica* 32 (1978), 125–130.

In large scale formal division the first movement follows a sonata allegro scheme, but once again the deviations are more interesting. The extent of the second theme boldly infringes upon the movement's proportions. Its revolving figuration is re-colored solely through harmony and exhibits that self-contained circularity which in its stasis is far removed from Beethoven's brand of goal-orientation. The two part main theme, unfolding on a moving tremolo background (which has often caused the work to be judged 'orchestral') corresponds to more orthodox sonata form, but Schubert brings to the comprehensive development less of his structural and more of his harmonic energies. The recapitulation, beginning with the reverse of the opening motto (this time g minor follows G major) is so much changed, varied and enlarged that its summarizing character fades against the impression of wide-ranging harmonic variety and individual activity. The *Andante un poco moto,* with a songlike layout, is different from the slow movements of the a minor and the d minor quartets in being full of inner dynamic and timbral oppositions. The b minor scherzo, comparable to that of the C major symphony, is characterized by a new kind of contrapuntal voice leading (very much subtler in comparison to the young works), as for example in the outer voices in the last third of the slow movement, and in the inversion and strettos of the scherzo theme.

Chromaticism and major-minor opposition also characterize the final movement. Analogous in character to that of the d minor quartet, it is built on a larger scale but at the same time is tighter in structure: "A movement of incomprehensible richness and, despite the appearance of boundlessly sweeping fantasy, of the greatest concision."[23]

23 Riezler, *loc. cit.,* 98.

The harmonic ambivalence gets its particular charm through the chromaticization of the middle voices and through the smooth and quick change of harmony. Thus, this movement unfolds not only in the realm of melody and rhythm, but also has some contrary harmonic components, and strives for phrase displacement, and free use of timbral and structural techniques, the full consequence of which was first realized in the twentieth century. Schubert's string quartets (in particular the last four), while smaller in quantity than the middle quartets of Beethoven, set standards for quartet composition in the nineteenth century. Their influence is found in Dvořák and Reger, in Bruckner and Hugo Wolf, and even in the young Schoenberg's D major quartet of 1897.

Discography

For many readers of this book, string quartet listening may be limited to the technical media, that is, to radio and recordings. Perhaps the reader lives in a medium size city, a small town or rural area where public concerts are rare, and such as there are never feature string quartets. Most likely home performance is impossible: the number of qualified amateur quartets is very limited, aside from the fact that the late Beethoven quartets or works written since the middle of the nineteenth century can hardly be performed without the skills of a professional musician. The following selected, chronological discography, with brief commentary, may provide some suggestions for building a collection. The judgments expressed are all a product of the listening experience of the author himself, who has regularly written reviews of new quartet recordings in trade periodicals since 1970. The selections here have been made throughout on the basis of musical interpretation and questions of technical perfection and production of the recordings have been intentionally ignored, as they are of less interest in this connection. Thus, technical standards have been considered with regard to the recordings' times of origin. Historical recordings (from the time before introduction of stereo) are mentioned occasionally.

The discography refers throughout to recordings that were available on the German market at time of publication (that is, in the summer of 1979). An exception has been made for recordings that can now only be gotten from antiquarians, though their re-release is recommended: these are listed separately. Since record numbers frequently change on account of re-releases, recombination, excerpts on cassette and price changes, the listing here is limited to the record companies. For the same reason price lists are not given.[1]

---

1 In order to save space, the names of the record companies will be abbreviated in the text in the usual way, as follows:

Ariola	Ariola-Eurodisc, Munich
BM	Bärenreiter-Musicaphon, Kassel
Bellaphon	Bellaphon Records, Frankfurt/Main
CBS	CBS Records, Frankfurt/Main
Colos	Colosseum Records, Nuremberg
DaCa	Da Camera Records, Mannheim
DG	Deutsche Grammophon Gesellschaft, Hamburg
Disco	Disco-Center, Kassel (Sales representative for Swedish, Hungarian and Polish recordings)
EMI	EMI-Electrola, Cologne
Fono	Fono Records, Münster (Marketing FSM, Candide, Vox)
Int	Intercord Music Company, Stuttgart
Phi	Phonogram (Philips) Records, Hamburg
RCA	RCA records, Hamburg
Tel	TELDEC-Telefunken-Decca Records, Hamburg
Wer	WERGO Records, Mainz

The Beginnings

While the great names in the history of the string quartet are very well represented on records today, the situation is much worse with regard to less well known composers. For the beginnings of the genre, that is, the time when compositional technique specific to the quartet was taking shape around 1750, one can — apart from Haydn and Boccherini — find one's way around only with difficulty. Two cassette releases offer some help: the Schäffer Quartet of Cologne released a cassette a few years ago entitled *The early string quartet in Europe* (Fono). Of the works in this collection only a few, by Michael Haydn, Giuseppe Cambini, Franz Xaver Richter, Giuseppe Tomasini, Giuseppe Nardini and Carl Dittersdorff can be considered genuine string quartets. Of particular interest here is the documentation (however small) of the northern Italian instrumental school around Sammartini. These recordings are expanded upon by three works in *Mannheim und Wien* (Tel) of the Vienna Concentus Musicus, with quartets by Richter, Mathias Georg Monn and Florian Gassmann.

Luigi Boccherini

In comparison with his compositional and historical importance for the genre, Luigi Boccherini is very much under-represented. At this time, the six op. 32 quartets by the Esterhazy quartet from Holland (Tel) are available in an acceptable but not high quality production on historical instruments. In addition, the op. 8 no. 5 and op. 33 no. 6 quartets have been recorded by the Dornbusch quartet of Frankfurt (DaCa), op. 39 by the Italian Quartetto Caecilia of Rome (DaCa), and the quartets op.

183

6 nos. 1 and 3, and op. 58 no. 2 by the Quartetto Italiano (Phi). The Italian recordings by the Carmirelli Quartet are virtually impossible to get in Germany.

Joseph Haydn

The recording situation for this 'father' of the string quartet has improved much in the last few years, thanks to the complete recording of all the authentic quartets by the English Aeolian Quartet (Tel). They are up to the music's considerable demands throughout and have in the meantime augmented the series with six cassettes. Here the early works in particular — the quartets op. 1, 2 and 9 — can be had for the first time in productions of satisfactory quality. The op. 17 quartets have been done very solidly and precisely by the Koeckert Quartet (DG), by the Ulbricht Quartet of Dresden (Ariola, now out of print), and, in a very careful and structurally clear interpretation, by the Juilliard Quartet (CBS). An outstanding rendition of the op. 33 cycle was produced by the (unfortunately now disbanded) Weller Quartet (Tel), and the young Tokyo String Quartet (DG) has recorded the op. 50 quartets stylistically and extremely well. The "Tost" quartets op. 54, 35 and 64, as well as the "Seven Words" op. 51 and the late quartets op. 71, 74 and 76, can be had in a performance by the Amadeus Quartet (DG), which here exhibits something of its better side. Op. 54 has been perfectly recorded, and with great inspiration, by the Juilliard Quartet (CBS). While there are hardly any alternatives to the recorded performances of the Aeolian Quartet for op. 71 and 74 things are better for op. 76 and op. 77. To be recommended here are the (rather old) recordings of the Amadeus Quartet (DG), two records with op. 64 no. 5 and op. 76 nos. 2—4 by the Quartetto Italiano

(Phi), the Heutling Quartet with op. 76 no. 3 and op. 77 no. 2 (EMI), the Alban Berg Quartet of Vienna with op. 74 no. 3 and op. 76 no. 3 (Tel), as well as the Melos Quartet with op. 20 no. 4, op. 33 no. 3 and op. 76 no. 3 and 4 (Int).

Wolfgang Amadeus Mozart

There are three complete recordings of Mozart's 23 string quartets: by the Heutling Quartet (EMI), the Quartetto Italiano (Phi) and the Amadeus Quartet (DG). The level of these interpretations is so high that personal taste and economy should be considered here. The ten "great" quartets, that is, the six Haydn quartets, the D major quartet KV 499 and the three Prussian quartets, have all been recorded by the Juilliard Quartet (CBS), whose performance of the Haydn quartets remains, for me, unsurpassed to this day. The Haydn quartets are also available complete in a similarly excellent production by the Melos quartet (DG). The four late quartets have also been recorded by the Melos quartet (Int) and by the Alban Berg Quartet (Tel), an ensemble of deep understanding and sensitivity, whose performance of the Haydn quartets likewise succeeds brilliantly.

Ludwig van Beethoven

With Ludwig van Beethoven there seems at first glance an almost dizzying number of recordings. Yet if one breaks it down and eliminates the many mediocre performances, the selection is not large at all. Complete recordings that are up to the very considerable technical and intellectual demands of these works are — in descending order of recommendation — the recordings by the

185

Juilliard Quartet (CBS), the Amadeus Quartet (DG), the Quartetto Italiano (Phi) and the Végh Quartet (Tel). The complete recording by the Guarneri Quartet (RCA) is unavailable at this time. A good addition to the complete recordings are the editions of early, middle or late quartets. Recordings of op. 18 that should be mentioned are those by the Borodin Quartet (Ariola) and the Bartók Quartet (Disco), and for op. 59 the old Hungarian String Quartet (EMI). The op. 74—95 quartets were recorded excellently (but are long out of print) by the Weller Quartet (Tel). The historical recording of the late Beethoven Quartets by the Busch Quartet (EMI) represents the highest standard of interpretation. Quite illuminating in clarification of structure are the performances of the La-Salle Quartet (DG), and certainly those of the Smetana Quartet (Ariola). Single recordings of the late quartets are for the most part extracts from a complete or partial edition.

Franz Schubert

A complete recording of all fifteen string quartets, on a high level throughout, is available by the Melos Quartet (DG). There is a partial recording (without the quartets no. 1—7), also excellent, by the Heutling Quartet (EMI). Otherwise, performances of the early or middle quartets — except for the g minor work D. 173 — are completely lacking. The late quartets (the c minor movement D. 703, the a minor quartet D. 804, the d minor work D. 810, and the G major quartet D. 889) have been recorded by the Juilliard Quartet (CBS), the Amadeus Quartet (DG) and the New Hungarian Quartet (Fono). Single recordings worthy of recommendation are the a minor with the Guarneri Quartet (RCA), the d minor with the Busch

Quartet (EMI-Historical) and the Cleveland Quartet (RCA) and, finally, the G major with the Tel Aviv Quartet (DaCa) and — almost unchanllenged — with the Bartholdy Quartet (EMI).

Other String Quartets between 1750 and 1830

The recording situation with moderately and less well known quartets of the classic era is in inverse proportion to their abundant diffusion in their day: only exceptionally can they be gotten on records. There are at this time no recorded performances of quartets by Albrechtsberger, Eybler, Förster, Krommer, Kozeluch, Gyrowetz, Pleyel, Hoffmeister, Romberg, Vanhall, Vorisek and Wranitzky. There are, however, in a cassette *Haydn, seine Freunde und Schüler* (EMI), one quartet each of Peter Haensel and Giuseppe Tomasini, and in single recordings by the Swedish Saulesco Quartet two works of Haydn's Swedish contemporary Johan Wikmanson (Disco). Valuable as a good example of the *"Quatuor d'airs inconnu"* style of writing is a quartet of Franz Danzi on themes of Mozart's Figaro performed by the Munich Sinnhoffer Quartet (Musica bavarica), along with a late string quartet in a minor op. 122 of Friedrich Kuhlau recorded by the Bartholdy Quartet of Karlsruhe (Armida).

Translator's Note to the Discography

The discography has been translated just as it was originally written. Naturally, not all these recordings or labels are available in the United States, so a brief report on the author's suggestions with reference to the American market has been made (in the summer of 1982). Readers are advised to check the latest *Schwann catalog* (revised monthly) for further recordings and current availability.

The Beginnings

Both anthologies mentioned have been released in the U.S.: that by the Schäffer Quartet on Vox and the Concentus Musicus on Tel.

Luigi Boccherini

The Esterhazy Quartet's recording is available on Tel, and the Quartetto Italiano on Phi. Two works (op. 39 no. 8 and op. 44 no. 4) performed by the Carmirelli Quartet are on Turnabout.

Joseph Haydn

The Aeolian Quartet's complete recording was issued in the U.S. on the London label. No separate recording of op. 17 is available. Of the recordings mentioned for op. 20, only that by the Juilliard Quartet (Columbia) is currently on the market. There is no complete recording in the U.S. of op. 33. The Tokyo String Quartet's performance of op. 50 is on DG. As for the recommended collection of several works by the Amadeus Quartet on DG, only op. 71 and 74 are currently available. Op. 51

and 54 are not represented, and op. 55 and 64 only in part. Nor is there any listing for a recording of op. 54 by the Juilliard Quartet. Recordings by the Amadeus Quartet and the Quartetto Italiano of op. 76 no. 3 can be had on DG and Phi respectively. The Heutling and Melos Quartets do not have U.S. releases, though the Alban Berg Quartet's recordings of op. 74 no. 3 and 76 no. 3 are available on Tel.

Wolfgang Amadeus Mozart

Of the complete recordings of Mozart's quartets, only that of the Amadeus Quartet on DG is available in America. There is nothing current by the Heutling Quartet, but most of the contributions of the Quartetto Italiano are available on Phi. Of the ten "great" quartets mentioned as recorded by the Juilliard Quartet, only four (KV 499, the three "Prussian" quartets KV 475, 489 and 490) are available on Columbia. The Melos' recording of the "Haydn" quartets is available on DG along with their performance of the last two quartets. There is a Tel release of the last four quartets with the Alban Berg Quartet.

Ludwig van Beethoven

All the complete recordings mentioned are available, though those of the Juilliard and Végh Quartets do not include op. 135. The Guarneri's recordings of all the middle and late quartets can be gotten in the U.S. on RCA. Nothing of the Borodin or Bartók Quartets is available for op. 18, though there are several other recordings, for example by the Hungarian Quartet on Seraphim (along with op. 59). There are no recordings by the

Weller, Busch or Smetana Quartets currently listed, but there are releases of the late quartets (op. 127—135) on DG by the LaSalle Quartet.

Franz Schubert

The Melos Quartet's complete recording is available. Complete recordings of the late quartets (D. 703 and following) are available only by the New Hungarian Quartet on Vox. The Guarneri Quartet's performances of D. 810 and D. 887 have been re-released in the U.S. on RCA; these works are also available by the Juilliard Quartet on CBS. No recordings by the Busch, Cleveland, Tel Aviv or Bartholdy Quartets are currently listed.

Other String Quartets between 1750 and 1830

None of the works or collections mentioned are available in the U.S., nor are there any recordings of quartets by the several composers mentioned.

Abbreviations

AfMw	Archiv für Musikwissenschaft
DTB	Denkmäler der Tonkunst in Bayern
JAMS	Journal of the American Musicological Society
Mf	Die Musikforschung
MGG	Die Musik in Geschichte und Gegenwart, ed. Friedrich Blume (Kassel & Basel, 1949–)
ML	Music and Letters
MQ	Musical Quarterly
MR	The Music Review
NMA	Neue Mozart Ausgabe (Kassel & Basel, 1968–)
NzfM	Neue Zeitschrift für Musik
ÖMZ	Österreichische Musikzeitschrift
Rass Mus	Rassegna musicale
RMI	Rivista musicale Italiana
StzMW	Studien zur Musikwissenschaft

Bibliography

Abert, Hermann: "Sechs unter Mozarts Namen neu aufgefundene Streichquartette" in *Mozart-Jahrbuch* 3 (1929), 9–58.

Abraham, Gerald: Beethoven's second-period quartets (2nd ed., London, 1943).

Adorno, Theodor W.: "Spätstil Beethoven" in *idem, Moments musicaux* (Frankfurt, 1964), 13–17; also in *Beethoven '70* (Frankfurt, 1972), 14–19.

Altmann, Wilhelm: *Handbuch für Streichquartettspieler*, 4 vols. (Berlin, 1928–1931; repr. 2 vols., Wilhelmshaven, 1972).

Arlt, Wulf: 'Aspekte des Gattungsbegriffs in der Musikgeschichtsschreibung' in *Gattungen der Musik: Festschrift für Leo Schrade* (Bern, 1973), 11–94.

Bäder, E. M.: 'Studien zu den Streichquartetten op. 1–33 von J. Haydn' (dissertation, Göttingen, 1945; typescript).

Baruch, Gerth-Wolfgang: *Beethovens Streichquartette* (Prague, 1938; Engl. transl., New York, 1938).

Barrett-Ayres, Reginald: *Joseph Haydn and the string quartet* (London, 1974).

Beck, Hermann: "Studien über das Tempoproblem bei Beethoven" (dissertation, Erlangen, 1954; typescript).

Benestad, Finn: "Mozarts strykekvartett in D-Dur (KV 575)" in *Norsk Musikkgranskning Arbok* 1959–1961 (Stockholm), 74–89.

Biamonti, Giovanni: *I quartetti di Beethoven* (Rome, 1924).

Blume, Friedrich: "J. Haydns künstlerische Persönlichkeit in seinen Streichquartetten" in *Jahrbuch Peters* 1931; also in *idem, Syntagma musicologicum*, vol. 1 (Kassel, 1963), 526–551.

Bonaccorsi, Alfredo: "Luigi Boccherini e il quartetto" in *Accademia Musicale Chigiana, Settimane Musicale* 19 (1962), 301–306.

Bonavia, F.: "Franz Schubert's chamber music" in *ML* 9 (1928), 368–371.

Bónis, Ferenc. "Csermák Antal kamaraseneje" (Csermak's chamber music) in *Uj zenei szemle* 3 (1952), No. 5, 10–15.

Borciani, Paolo: *Il Quartetto* (Milan, 1973); introduction to the technique of quartet playing.

Breh, Karl: "Streichquartette im Workshop. Bericht über einen Versuch" in *Hifi-Stereophonie* 13 (1973), 260–266.

Broyles, Michael E: "Beethoven's sonata op. 14, no. 1 — originally for strings?" in *JAMS* 23 (1970), 405ff.

Bruce, I. M.: "Notes from an analysis of Mozart's quartet in G major K. 387" in *MR* 10 (1949), 97–110.

Chailley, Jacques: "Sur la signification du quator de Mozart K 465, dit 'les dissonances' et du 7ème quator de Beethoven" in *Natalicia Musicologica* (1962), 283–292 (Jeppesen Festschrift).

Cherbuliez, Antonie-Elysee: "Zur harmonischen Analyse der Einleitung in Mozarts C-Dur Quartett (KV 465)" in *Bericht über die mus. Tagugn der Int. Stiftung Mozarteum August 1931* (Leipzig, 1932), 103–111.

—: "Bemerkungen zu den 'Haydn'-Streichquartetten Mozarts und Haydns 'Russischen' Streichquartetten" in *Mozart-Jahrbuch* (1959).

Chusid, Martin: "The chamber music of Franz Schubert" (dissertation, Berkeley, 1961).

Ciortea, Tudor: *Cvartetele de Beethoven* (Bucharest, 1968).

Clark, Rebecca: "The history of the viola in quartet writing" in *ML* 4 (1923), 6–17.

Cobbett, W. W., ed.: *Cyclopedic survey of chamber music,* 2 vols., with supplementary material by Colin Mason (London 1929; 2nd ed., London, 1963).

Cooke, Deryck: "The unity of Beethoven's late quartets" in *MR* 24 (1963), 30–49.

Dahlhaus, Carl: *Grundlagen der Musikgeschichte* (Cologne, 1977).

—: *Die Idee der absoluten Musik* (Kassel, 1978).

—: "Was ist eine musikalische Gattung?" in *NZfM* 135 (1974), 620–625.

—: "La Malinconia" (on Beethoven's op. 18 no. 6) in *Beethoven (Wege der Forschung),* ed. Ludwig Finscher (Darmstadt, in preparation).

—: "Über Schuberts Sonatenform: der erste Satz des G-Dur Quartetts D. 887" in *Musica* 32 (1978), 125—130.

—: "Schuberts frühe Streichquartette" in *Kongressbericht Schubert-Kongress 1978* (Vienna, in preparation).

Dent, Edward J.: "The earliest string quartets" in *Monthly Musical Record* 33 (1903).

Deutsch, Otto Erich: "The chronology of Schubert's string quartets" in *ML* 24 (1943), 25—30.

Dittersdorf, Carl Ditters von: *Lebensbeschreibung* (autobiography), ed. N. Miller (Munich, 1967).

Doflein, Erich: "Historismus und Historisierung in der Music" in *Festschrift Walter Wiora* (Kassel, 1967), 43ff.

Dunhill, Thomas F.: *Mozart's string quartets* (London, 1927; Westport, Conn., 1970).

Ebert, Alfred: "Die erste Aufführung von Beethovens Es-Dur Quarop. 127 im Frühling 1825" in *Die Musik* 9 (1910), 42—63, 90—106.

Elst, Nancy van der: "Een Studie over Beethovens laatste Strijkkwartetten" in *Mens en Melodie* 20 (1965), 274—276.

Elvers, Rudolf: "Ein unbekannter Entwurf zum Menuett des Jagd-Quartetts" (Mozart KV 458) in *Mitteilungen der ISM 1956, No. 18*, 2—5.

Engel, Hans: "Haydn, Mozart und die Klassik" in *Mozart-Jahrbuch* (1959), 46—79.

Essner, W.: "Die Thematik der Menuette in den Streichquartetten J. Haydns" (dissertation, Erlangen, 1923; typescript).

Ferguson, Donald N.: *Image and structure in chamber music* (London, 1964).

Finscher, Ludwig: *Studien zur Geschichte des Streichquartetts* I (Kassel, 1974).

—: "Streichquartett" in *MGG*, vol. 12, cols. 1559—1601.

—: "Zur Sozialgeschichte des klassischen Streichquartetts" in *Kongress-Bericht Kassel* (1962).

—: "Mozarts Mailänder Streichquartette" in *Mf* 19 (1966).

—: "Haydn und das italienische Streichquartett" in *Analecta Musicologica* 4 (1967), 13—37.

—: "Hausmusik und Kammermusik" in *Festschrift Karl Vötterle* (Kassel, 1968).

—: "Beethovens Streichquartett op. 59, 3. Versuch einer Interpretation" in G. Schumacher ed., *Zur musikalischen Analyse* (Darmstadt, 1974), 122—160.

—: "Mozarts erstes Streichquartett: Lodi, 15 März 1770" in *Analecta musicologica* 18 (1978), 246—270.

Fischer, W.: "Zur Entwicklungsgeschichte des Wiener klassischen Stils" in *StzMW* 3 (1915).

Fiske, Roger: *Beethoven's last quartets* (London, 1940; 3rd ed., 1948).

Forchert, Arno: "Die Darstellung der Melancholie in Beethoven's op. 18,6" in *Beethoven,* ed. Ludwig Finscher (Darmstadt, in preparation).

Geiringer, Karl: *Joseph Haydn* (Mainz, 1959).

Gerard, Yves: *Thematic, bibliographical and critical catalogue of the works of Luigi Boccherini* (London, 1969).

Gerbert, Rudolf: "Harmonische Probleme in Mozarts Streichquartetten" in *Mozart-Jahrbuch* 2 (1924), 55—77.

Germann, J.: "Die Entwicklung der Exposition in J. Haydns Streichquartetten" (dissertation, Bern, 1964; typescript).

Gillett, Judy: "The problem of Schubert's G major string quartet D. 887" in *MR* 35 (1974), 281—291.

Grew, Sidney, "The 'Great Fugue': an analysis" in *ML* 12 (1931), 253—261.

Griesinger, G. A.: "Biographische Notizen über J. Haydn" in *Allgemeine Musikalische Zeitung* 9 (1809).

Gülke, Peter: "Introduktion als Widerspruch im System" (on op. 59 no. 3) in *Jahrbuch Peters* (1970), 5—40.

Hecker, Joachim von: "Untersuchungen an den Skizzen zu op. 131 von L. v. Beethoven" (dissertation, Freiburg, 1956; typescript).

Helm, Theodor: *Beethovens Streichquartette* (Leipzig, 1885; 2nd ed., 1910; 3rd ed., 1921).

Hemel, Victor van: *de kamermusiek* (3rd ed., Antwerp, 1965).

Herter Norton, M. D.: *String quartet playing* (New York, 1925).

—: *The art of string quartet playing, technique and interpretation* (new ed. of the preceding, London, 1963).

Heuss, Alfred: *Kammermusikabende* (Leipzig, 1919).

Hinderberger, Adolf: "Die Motivik in Haydns Streichquartetten" (dissertation, Bern, 1935; typescript).

Hughes, Rosemary: *Haydn's string quartets* (BBC Guides, London, 1956).

Hull, A. Eaglefield: "The earliest known string quartet" in *MQ* 15 (1929).

Huschke, Konrad: *Das Siebengestirn der Schubert'schen Kammermusikwerke* (Pritzwalk, 1928).

d'Indy, Vincent: *Analyse des 17 Quatuors de Beethoven, texte recueilli et rédigé par P. Coindreau* (Paris, 1909).

Jokl, E.: "Die letzten Streichquartette Beethovens" (dissertation, Vienna, 1905; typescript).

Johnson, Douglas: "Beethoven's sketches for the scherzo of the quartet op. 18 no. 6" in *JAMS* 23 (1970), 385–404.

Keller, Hans: "The Interpretation of the Haydn quartets" in *The Score* 24 (1958), 14–35.

Kerman, Joseph: *The Beethoven Quartets* (London, 1967).

King, Alexander Hyatt: "Mozart's Counterpoint" in *ML* 26 (1945).

—: "Mozart's Prussian quartets in relation to his style" in *ML* 21 (1940), 328–346.

Kirkendale, Warren: *Fuge und Fugato in der Kammermusik des Rokoko und der Klassik* (Tutzing, 1966).

—: "The 'Great Fuge' op. 133: Beethoven's Art of Fugue" in *Acta Musicologica* 35 (1963), 14–24.

Klinkhammer, Rudolf: *Die langsame Einleitung in der Instrumentalmusik der Klassik und Romantik* (Regensburg, 1971).

Klockow, Erich: "Die ersten drei Haydn gewidmeten Streichquartette" in *Mitteilungen für die Mozart-Gemeinde in Berlin*, No. 43 (1925), 3–26.

—: "Mozarts Streichquartett in A-Dur (KV 464)" *Mozart-Jahrbuch* 3 (1929), 209–241.

—: "Mozarts Streichquartett in C-Dur (KV 465)" in *Deutsche Musikkultur* 6 (1941–1942), 67–75.

Kolisch, Rudolf: "Tempo and character in Beethoven's music" in *MQ* 29 (1943), 169–187, 291–312.

Kolneder, Walter: "Zur Vorgeschichte des Streichquartetts" in *Hifi-Stereophonie* 13 (1974), 266–268.

Kopfermann, Michael: *Beiträge zur musikalischen Analyse später Werke Ludwig van Beethovens* (Munich, 1975).

Kornauth, Egon: "Die thematische Arbeit in J. Haydns Streichquartetten seit 1780" (dissertation, Vienna, 1915; typescript).

Kramarz, Joachim: *Das Streichquartett* (Wolfenbüttel, 1961), *Beiträge zur Schulmusik, 9*.

Kramer, Jonathan D.: "Multiple and non-linear time in Beethoven's op. 135" in *Perspectives of New Music* 11 (1973).

Kreft, Ekkehard: *Die späten Quartette Beethovens* (Bonn, 1964).

Kroher, Ekkehard: "Die Polyphonie in den Streichquartetten Mozarts und Haydns" in *Wiss. Zeitschrift der Universität Leipzig* (1955—1956), 369—387, *Ges. und Sprachwiss.*, ser. 5.

Kropfinger, Klaus: "Zur thematischen Funktion der langsamen Einleitung bei Beethoven" in *Festschrift J. Schmidt-Görg* (Bonn, 1967), 197—216.

La Laurencie, L. de: *L'ecole francaise de violon de Lully à Viotti*, 3 vols. (Paris, 1922—1924).

Landon, H. C. Robbins: "On Haydn's quartets op. 1 and 2" in *MR* 13 (1952), 181ff.

—: "Doubtful and spurious quartets and quintets attributed to Haydn" in *MR* 18 (1957).

La Rue, Jan: "Dittersdorf negotiates a price" in *H. Albrecht in memoriam* (Kassel, 1962).

Leclair, S. L.: "The chamber music of F. Schubert" in *MQ* 14(1928), 515—528).

Lehmann, Ursula: *Deutsche und italienisches Wesen in der Vorgeschichte des klassischen Streichquartetts* (Würzburg, 1939).

Leichentritt, Hugo: *Musikalische Formenlehre* (2nd ed., Leipzig, 1950), 330—332, 350—358 (on Beethoven's op. 130 and 133).

Leuchter, E.: "Die Kammermusikwerke Florian Leopold Gassmanns" (dissertation, Vienna, 1926; typescript).

Linde, Bernard van der: *Die unorthographische Notation in Beethovens Klaviersonaten und Streichquartetten* (Vienna, 1962); excerpts in *Beethoven-Studien* (Vienna, 1970), 271—325.

Lippmann, Friedrich and Ludwig Finscher: "Die Streichquartettmanuskripte der Bibliothek Doria-Pamphily in Rom" in *Analecta Musicologica* 9 (1969), 120—133.

Lonchamps, Jacques: *Les Quatuors a cordes de Beethoven* (Paris, 1956).

MacArdle, Donald W.: "Beethoven's quartet in B flat op. 130. An analysis" in *MR* 8 (1947), 11—14.

—: "The Artaria editions of Beethoven's C major quartet" in *JAMS* 16 (1963), 254—257.

Mahaim, Ivan: *E. Ysaye et les "Derniers Quatuors" de Beethoven* (Geneva, 1958).

—. *Beethoven. Naissance et renaissance des derniers quatuors*, 2 vols. (Paris, 1964).

Marliave, Joseph de: *Les Quatuors de Beethoven* (Paris, 1925; engl. transl. New York, 1961).

Mann, Carl-Heinz: "Formale Probleme in den späten Werken Beethovens. Untersuchungen zum Stil der Kammermusik und des Klavierwerks" (dissertation, Cologne, 1955; typescript).

Marx, Adolf Bernhard: *Die Lehre von der musikalischen Komposition*, vol. 4 (Leipzig, 1847).

Mersmann, Heinrich: *Die Kammermusik*, in H. Kretzschmar, *Führer durch den Konzertsaal*, part 3 (Leipzig, 1930–1933).

Mies, Paul: "Bemerkungen zu Beethovens Notation mit Beispielen aus den späten Streichquartetten" in *Sbornik praci filosoficki fakulty brnenske university* 14 (1965), No. 9, 161–165.

Mila, Massimo: *I quartetti di Beethoven*, 2 vols. (Turin, 1968–1969).

Misch, Ludwig: "Das Finale des C-Dur quartetts op. 59,3. Eine Formstudie" in *idem, Beethoven-Studien* (Bonn, 1950), 36–41.

Mishkin, Henry G.: "Five autograph string quartets by G. B. Sammartini in *JAMS* 6 (1953), 136–147.

Moe, Orin: "Texture in the string quartets of Haydn to 1787" (dissertation, University of California at Santa Barbara, 1970; microfilm).

—: "Texture in Haydn's string quartets' in *MR* 35 (1974), 4–22.

Moldenhauer, Hans: "Busonis Kritik an den letzten Streichquartetten Beethovens" in *NZfM* 121 (1960), 416–417.

Newman, William S.: *The sonata in the classic era* (Chapel Hill, 1963).

Nikolaeva, N.: "Vzgljad v buduscee" (A look into the future.) in *Sovetskaja Muzyka* 31 (1967), No. 2, 120–128; on Beethoven's late quartets.

Orel, Alfred: "Das Autograph des Scherzos aus Beethovens Streichquartett op. 127" in *Festschrift Hans Engel* (Kassel, 1964), 274–280.

Palm, Albert: "Mozarts Streichquartett d-moll (KV 421) in der Interpretation Momignys" in *Mozart-Jahrbuch* (1962–1963), 256–279.

—: "Unbekannte Haydn-Analysen" in *Haydn Yearbook* 4 (1968), 169–194.

Pankaskie, Lewis Vincent: "Tonal Organization in the sonata form movements in Haydn's string quartets" (dissertation, University of Michigan, Ann Arbor, 1957; typescript).

Pecman, Rudolf: "Pravuc pisnovy sbornik z roku 1790 a' Razumovske kvartety' Ludwiga van Beethovena" in *Shornik praci filosoické fakulty brnenske university* 6 (1957), No. 1, 53—63.

—: *Beethovenovy smyccové kvartety* (Brno, 1970).

Pincherle, Marc: *Feuillets d'histoire du violon* (Paris, 1927).

—: "On the origins of the string quartet" in *MQ* 15 (1929).

—: *Les instruments du quator* (Paris, 1948).

Pochon, A.: *A progressive method of string quartet playing* (New York, 1924).

Radcliffe, Philip: *Beethoven's string quartets* (2nd ed., London, 1978).

Randall, J. K.: "Haydn: string quartet in D major, op. 76, no. 5" in *MR* 21 (1960), 94—105.

Ratz, Erwin: 'Die Original Fassung des B-Dur Streichquartetts op. 130/133 (Beethoven)" in *ÖMZ* 7 (1952), 81—87.

—: *Einführung in die musikalische Formenlehre* (2nd ed., Vienna, 1968).

Reed, Carl H.: "Motivic unity in selected keyboard sonatas and string quartets of Joseph Haydn" (dissertation, University of Washington, 1966).

Reti, Rudolph: *The thematic process in music* (London, 1961).

Riemann, Hugo: *Beethovens Streichquartette* (Berlin, 1903).

—: "Mannheimer Kammermusik des 18. Jahrhunderts," introduction to *Denkmäler der Tonkunst in Bayern* XV (Leipzig, 1914).

Rieseling, Robert A.: "Motivic structures in Beethoven's last quartets" in *Paul A. Pisk. Essays in his honor* (Austin, Texas, 1966), 141—162.

Riezler, Walter: *Schuberts Instrumentalmusik. Werkanalysen.* (Zurich, 1967).

Rigler, Gertrude: "Die Kammermusik von Dittersdorf" in *StzMW* 14 (1927), 179—212.

Rolland, Romain: *Les derniers Quators* (Paris, 1943; 2nd ed., 1966).

Roncaglia, Gino: "Di G. G. Cambini, quartettista padre" in *Rass. Mus.* 6 (1933).

—: "G. G. Cambini, quartettista romantico" in *Rass. Mus.* 7 (1934).

200

—: "G. G. Cambini quartettista" in *Accademia Musicale Chigiana Settimana Musicale* 19 (1962), 293—299.

Sachse, Hans-Martin: "Franz Schuberts Streichquartette" (dissertation, Münster, 1958).

Saint-Fox, George de: "Le derniers quatuor de Mozart (KV 590)" in *Studien zur Musikforschung. Festschrift Guido Adler* (Vienna, 1930), 168—173.

Salvetti, Guido: "Luigi Boccherini nell'ambito del quartetto italiano del secondo Settecento" in *Analecta Musicologica* 12 (1973), 227—252.

Sandberger, Adolf: "Zur Geschichte des Haydn'schen Streichquartetts" in *Altbayerische Monatsschrift* 2 (1900); expanded in *idem*, *Ausgew. Aufsätze zur Musikgeschichte*, vol. 1 (Munich, 1921).

Sauzay, E.: *Haydn, Mozart, Beethoven. Etude sur le quatuor* (Paris, 1861).

Schenker, Heinrich: "Beethoven zu seinem opus 127" in *Der Tonwille* 4 (1924), 39—41.

Scherchen, Hermann: "Beethovens grosse Fuge op. 133" in *Die Musik* 20 (1927—1928), 401—420; also in G. Schumacher, ed., *Zur musikalischen Analyse* (Darmstadt, 1974).

Schering, Arnold: *Beethoven und die Dichtung* (Berlin, 1936).

—: *Beethoven in neuer Deutung. I: Die Shakespeare-Quartette op. 95—131* (Leipzig, 1934).

Schlüter, P.: *Die Anfänge des modernen Streichquartetts* (Merseburg, 1939).

Schmid, H. K.: "Franz Schuberts neuentdecktes Streichquartett D. 96" in *AfMW* 1 (1918), 183—188.

Scott, Marion: "Haydn's op. 2 and op. 3" in *Proceedings of the Royal Musical Association* 61 (1934—1935).

Serrins, D.: "The validity of textbook concepts of 'sonata form' in the late string quartets of Haydn and Mozart' (dissertation, University of North Carolina, 1950; typescript).

Silbert, D.: "Ambiguity in the string quartets of Haydn" in *MQ* 36 (1950).

Sólyom, G.: "A klasszikus szazadforduló" in *Haydn Emlékére* (Budapest, 1960).

Somfai, László: "Zur Echtheitsfrage der Haydn'schen 'Opus 3' " in *Haydn Yearbook* 3 (1965), 153—165.

—: "A klasszikus kvartetthangiás megszületése Haydn vonósnegyeseibens" (The rise of the classical quartet sound in the string quartets of Haydn) in *Haydn Emlékére* (Budapest, 1960).

Sondheimer, Robert: *Haydn. A historical and psychological study based on his quartets* (London, 1951).

Stephan, Rudolf: "Zu Beethovens letzten Quartetten" in *Mf* 23 (1970), 245–256.

Stoeving, C. H. P.: *The violin, cello and string quartet* (New York, 1927).

van der Straeten, E.: "Schuberts Behandlung der Streichinstrumente mit besonderer Berücksichtigung der Kammermusik" in *Schubert-Kongress Berlin* 1928, 133–140.

Tertis, Lionel: "The string quartet" in *ML* 31 (1950), 148–150.

Torrefranca, Fausto: "J. W. A. Stamitz e il Prof. H. Riemann," chapter within "La creazione della Sonata dramatica moderna" in *Revista Musicale Italiana* 17 (1910), 351–358.

—: "La lotta per l'egemonia musicale nel settecento" in *Revista Musicale Italiana* 24 (1917); and 25 (1918).

—: "Avviamento alla storia del quartetto italiano" in *L'Approdo musicale,* 23 (1966).

Tovey, Donald Francis: *Essays and lectures on music* (London, 1949); analysis of op. 131.

Trimpert, Dieter Lutz: *Die quator concertants von Giuseppe Cambini* (Tutzing, 1967).

Truscott, Harold: "Schubert's d minor string quartet" in *MR* 19 (1958), 27–36.

—: "Schubert's string quartet in G major" in *MR* 20 (1959), 119–145.

Tyson, Alan and H. C. Robbins Landon: "Who composed Haydn's op. 3?" in *The Musical Times* (1964).

Ulrich, Homer: *Chamber music* (2nd ed., New York, 1966).

Unverricht, Hubert: *Die beiden Hofstetter* (Mainz, 1968).

Vetter, Walter: "Das Stilproblem in Beethovens op. 59" in *Mythos-Mens-Musica. Ges. Aufsätze zur Musikgeschichte* I (Leipzig, 1957).

Webster, James: "The chronology of Haydn's string quartets" in *MQ* 61 (1975), 17–46.

Wedig, Hans J.: *Beethovens Streichquartett op. 18,1 und seine erste Fassung* (Bonn, 1922).

Westrup, Jack Allan: *Schubert's chamber music*. (BBC music guides, London, 1969).

Windberger, Jacques: "Versuch über Beethovens letzte Streichquartette" in *Schweizerische Musikzeitung* (1970), 1–8.

Index